Better Behaviour through Golden Time

Colleg
rce C tr

Jenny Mosley and Helen Sonnet

Researcher: Dr Zara Gregory

Permission to photocopy

This book contains materials which may be reproduced by photocopier or other means for use by the purchaser. The permission is granted on the understanding that these copies will be used within the educational establishment of the purchaser. The book and all its contents remain copyright. Copies may be made without reference to the publisher or the licensing scheme for the making of photocopies operated by the Publishers Licensing Agency.

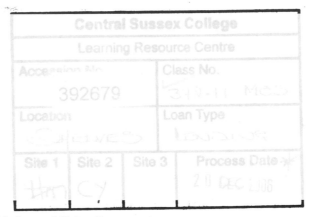
Better Behaviour through Golden Time
LL07059
ISBN 1 85503 394 1
© Jenny Mosley and Helen Sonnet
Photography © Brian Kingston and George Solomonides
Illustrations © Mark Cripps
All rights reserved
First published 2005

Printed in China for LDA
Abbeygate House, East Road, Cambridge, CB1 1DB

Acknowledgements

Thank you to the headteachers, teachers and teaching assistants at the many 'golden schools' who contributed to this book. They willingly provided information, wrote anecdotes and case studies, and generously shared aspects of their wonderfully insightful practice with us. We really, really value these schools for providing us with valuable feedback on the model and for persevering in making their schools better places for all. To make time when you are all so busy is truly amazing.

In particular, I should like to thank all the staff and children at the following schools: Birley Spa Community Primary School, Sheffield; Nyland School, Swindon; Blackwell Primary School, Derbyshire; Allanton Primary School, Shotts, North Lanarkshire; Marion Richardson School, Stepney, London; Stourfield First School, Bournemouth; Broadstone First School, Dorset; Cramond School, Edinburgh; Northwood School, Isle of Wight; Phoenix Secondary and Primary School, London; St Timothy's School, Coatbridge, Scotland; and Maplesdon Noakes School, Maidstone, Kent. These schools continue to develop their vision and practice on the Quality Circle Time model in a very creative and exciting way.

Thanks to Westfield First School, Berkhampsted, Hertfordshire; Kinson Primary School, Bournemouth; King's Furlong Infants School, Basingstoke; Sacred Heart Catholic Primary School, Coventry; Ashley Road Primary School, Aberdeen; Talavera Infants School, Aldershot; and Roseburn Primary School, Edinburgh, for being so open to working on new ideas and for persevering.

One school that we have worked particularly closely with is Bransgore School. This golden school has really taken Circle Time and Golden Time to its heart. It is a place where children and staff have Circle Time and everyone enjoys Golden Assemblies and peaceful and welcoming dining hall and playground areas decorated with golden displays. We are very grateful to the staff and pupils for all their support, including with photography sessions of their wonderful practice. Bransgore School is shortly to start work in circles with parents, and has developed many golden initiatives.

Thanks too to the thousands of other schools doing Golden Time in creative and sustained ways. I am sorry we couldn't write to you all to request your stories and case studies, but you know who you are!

Thank you to Helen Peter, one of our consultants, and to photographer Brian Kingston, who worked together during inspired photography sessions. A big thank you to our whole team of consultants who bravely develop our model in thousands of schools. You are great role models of positivity, endurance and whole-hearted vision.

And thank you to the National College for School Leadership – in particular the Talking Heads team, who provide an excellent forum for headteachers to communicate with key people in a website discussion community. I have had the pleasure of chatting on-line with numerous inspired headteachers about the behaviour and relationships of staff and pupils. Having sat in four of the hotseats, I thoroughly recommend that all heads avail themselves of this exciting forum.

We cannot give our thanks and acknowledgements without mentioning the backbone of the organisation. The administrative staff in our office are always beavering away, helping to organise. They are now too numerous to name everyone there, but we really value your support.

Thank you to Zara. You have really pulled this book together by going that bit deeper every time. Without your wonderful tenacity, intelligence and research abilities we would not have the vivid cameos from schools and children. You combine your own work with complementary therapies for children and research for our team with flair, good judgement and a lot of wisdom.

And lastly, thank you to Corin, our editor, for working so closely, patiently and creatively with us. Catherine, Carole and Jayne, also from LDA, are wonderful supporters of the model and are always very encouraging, insightful and fun to be with.

A profound thank you to the Findhorn Community, who asked me to speak at a conference on 'Healing the Soul of Education'. I recommend every tired teacher visits this community to refresh their spirit.

Jenny Mosley

Contents

Foreword

The main task of primary schools is to ensure as many children as possible achieve high standards, especially in literacy and numeracy, which underpin learning across the curriculum at secondary level and beyond.

Over the last few years, both as Secretary of State for Education and Employment and as Home Secretary, I have visited many schools. I am constantly struck by the importance of building a strong school ethos.

Those schools which expect high standards of behaviour, which insist on respect for and between all the individuals of the school community and which encourage children to make a contribution to improving the lives of others, also expect high academic standards. In short, they bring the best out in people.

This is easy to write in a foreword but requires great commitment and skill from heads, teachers and their staff in the schools that succeed.

This book provides practical guidance for school staff on how to achieve high standards of behaviour. I've seen the concept of Golden Time in operation in schools I've visited and been impressed by the difference it makes.

The Golden Rules are simple, common sense but every teacher knows that ensuring every child abides by them in the modern world is a constant challenge. This book, which is full of case studies, will help teachers meet that challenge.

In fact, when I read through the Golden Rules – which include 'We listen to people', 'We don't waste time' and 'We don't interrupt' – I thought I might seek to promote them in the House of Commons too! Whether this would work, I don't know. I do know, however, that in primary schools where these rules are followed, the lives of both children and teachers become more rewarding and productive.

David Blunkett
Home Secretary
August 2004

Preface

Having taught for fourteen years, I went freelance with the Whole School Quality Circle Time model in 1986. Thousands of schools and millions of shared ideas later, we – a small, brave and creative company – are still going strong! We have pioneered a range of highly acclaimed projects and resources to help create happier staffrooms, classrooms and playgrounds. Currently, we are working with the Primary National Strategy (thanks to Jean Gross) to make clear how our model fits into the three waves of their exciting and visionary strategy.

What is the learning on the way? Too huge – I need to write another book on the journey itself.

I have a profound, deep respect for many staff in schools. I know that teaching is a deeply spiritual job. You endlessly have to learn to be unconditional in your warmth to all children, to forgive the emotional onslaught they may throw at you and come back into school daily with a fresh and open outlook – taking care to leave yesterday's difficulties and hurts behind you.

What an amazing daily task! The only way you can be equal to it is to make sure you keep your own spirit high. In other words, you must not let your own inner light or energy become drained or dimmed out by the often overpowering emotional, behavioural and cognitive needs of the children.

You have a duty to yourself and all children to struggle to maintain your own emotional, creative, physical, cognitive and spiritual health. Making time for your needs is a prerequisite for becoming a good, sound teacher as it ensures you build up the inner strength and reserves to keep going and to model fun, joy and laughter for your children. Life is too short to allow yourself to lose your own vibrancy of spirit.

It's easy for me to preach this – now, having stopped being a class teacher, I just dash in and out of your schools. The people who have the daily barrage are truly the superheroes of our time. My consultants and I, through our journeys, meet many, many superheroes – smiling, warm people with a life outside their job. So, look after yourselves first!

Jenny Mosley

Introduction

Can you identify with these scenarios? Does your school need to find a solution to these problems? If so, then this is the book that will help you.

Picture these scenarios

'It's not my fault,' thought Ahmed angrily. 'Sakira and John started it first. She always picks on me. I hate school and I hate teachers. Bossy old cow.'

Hannah glanced out of the window. She could just see the top of the skipping rope flash up. 'It's always the same. I get on quietly with my work, do all my homework 'cos Mum and Dad keep on at me how important it is. The only break I get is at playtime. But this is the third time this week we've been kept in. Will it be like this always?'

Mr Drackett carried on guillotining the display cards. 'Being a TA gives you ulcers,' he decided. 'You can't speak up without thinking carefully over who you're offending. Some of these kids need to get in the fresh air. If we have wet play at lunchtime, I daren't think what the afternoon will be like.'

Mrs Khan glanced at the clock. She thought, 'Susheila should be back now. Poor little sweetheart, she had a tummy ache before going off to school. We love a quiet house, she and I. She can't bear the shouting that goes on in the class. She has been really on edge this week and very pale.'

Mr Jones took a sharp intake of breath. 'Oh great! Look at the line of kids outside my office. Why the hell can't the teachers sort it out themselves? I'll be late home again and too late again to take Jamie swimming. I don't know how much longer things can go on like this!'

Miss Simms looked at the clock and thought, 'Oh no! It will be Golden Time soon and half the class are going to have to watch the sand timer. What a disaster!'

How to use this book

This book has been written as a practical resource, at the same time providing some background to the initiatives. It provides a whole-school model for better behaviour. However, the model can also be implemented on a classroom basis.

Many of you will not have time to read this book from cover to cover immediately, but you can home in on selected chapters to get straightforward advice on how to start Golden Time and make it a success from day 1. However, Golden Time is not a panacea or a quick fix, and will take real dedication and effort. When carried out with conviction, it will save you and your class more time and energy than you expend, with the added advantage of helping with opportunities to boost children's self-esteem.

In several sections we have included key questions in the form of a checklist. Sometimes we felt that the rationale behind a question needed to be highlighted. We have done this in the form of an italicised sentence after the question. Other questions, we felt, were self-explanatory.

1

Why write a book about Golden Time?

Matthew's story

One Friday afternoon I ended up taking a pupil to A & E after a bad fall on our climbing frame during the lunch break. He had landed on his arm and was in obvious intense pain.

During the hospital visit the process of checking his injuries led to distressed yelps from the pupil as the doctors handled his arm. At one point he suddenly burst into tears. When I tried to console him and ask if he was OK, he replied, 'I'm missing my Golden Time!'

Geoff Mawson, Headteacher,
Birley Spa Community Primary School, Sheffield

A little background

School can be the most amazing place on earth to be or it can be a frustrating, exhausting black hole for your energy, creativity and confidence. You may arrive on a daily basis brimming with sunshine and goodwill, and yet within minutes a child's poor behaviour reduces you to an exasperated, shrieking nag. Enter Golden Time.

Golden Time is a fantastic positive behaviour-management system in its own right, much appreciated by children and adults up and down the country. Those involved in it know that:

- it works;
- it is manageable;
- when carried out properly, it carries on working;
- when done well, it can be wonderful.

Originally, Golden Time was developed as part of a systemic model, the Whole School Quality Circle Time model, highlighted in *All Round Success* (Mosley, 1989), and outlined in *Turn Your School Round* (Mosley, 1993) and *Quality Circle Time* (Mosley, 1996). It has been tested and used up and down the country for years now, and it is rooted in sound psychological theory. You do not have to take our word for that; the evidence runs throughout this book.

This book aims to:

- set out clearly what Golden Time is;
- describe how to set up Golden Time and, importantly, how to keep it running successfully;
- provide a summary of potentials and pitfalls of Golden Time, in order that you can make the very most of this simple but effective strategy;
- supply lots of exciting ideas and suggestions to enhance the ethos in which Golden Time can thrive and prosper most successfully;
- offer anecdotes, tips and case studies to refer to;
- provide ideas on how to vary Golden Time to suit your children – for example, when working with early-years children, children with special needs or certain children who you feel are 'beyond' this type of strategy;
- describe how to create the type of classroom where Golden Time will flourish, with tips for success to encourage new teachers and to serve as a reminder for those who are more experienced.

> Jenny Mosley's . . . work embodies some of the most important principles established by the Committee of Enquiry into Discipline in Schools set up in 1988 under my chairmanship. Our recommendations were published, as the Elton Report, in 1989.
>
> A central group of those recommendations urged every school to develop a 'whole school behaviour policy' involving, and supported by, everyone
>
> ➔

directly involved with the school itself. This theme has been central to Jenny Mosley's work in the field . . . Her scheme embraces a number of our other recommendations as well.

It has been very encouraging to hear, from many witnesses, of the success of her work in improving good schools and 'turning round' those in difficulty, as it endorses some of the Committee's most important findings . . .

Lord Elton

Golden Time as a strategy in its own right

Golden Time has become a key strategy for rewarding and celebrating behavioural success. Below are the main reasons for presenting this new book about it:

- To overcome the challenges that society has a tendency to hurl at teachers, teachers have reached out to grasp sound strategies to support them in managing the vast range of social, emotional and behavioural needs they now find within their classrooms.
- Good news travels very fast among teachers, and news of the success of Golden Time as a strategy has spread as fast as its use.
- This 'good' news has been passed mostly by word of mouth, which has led to its dilution as a strategy in many cases. Many pieces of the jigsaw puzzle are left out and the whole picture is flawed in many schools.
- Many teachers need to understand the psychology underpinning the practice in order to revitalise what may have become Rusty Time rather than Golden Time!

Golden Time works best when it is:

- made clear to children that it is linked to the school's Golden Rules;
- a well-organised session, not a run-down Friday afternoon session in which children play with puzzles with pieces missing and old computer paper, while the teacher hurriedly marks books and finishes a coffee in a corner of the room;

- built up with the children, so that everyone knows that it is a community celebration of the school's values.

Where Golden Time works in these ways, it can have the sort of impact seen in the illustration that follows.

> *If Golden Time is seen as a unique force in its own right and is placed at the heart of a school's positive behaviour, PSHE, citizenship and self-esteem policies, then it has potential to help schools release excellence.*

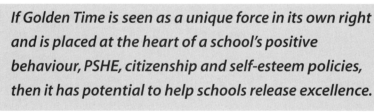

Blackwell Primary School
Primrose Hill
Blackwell
Derbyshire
21st March 2003

Dear Everyone at Jenny Mosley Consultancies,

We have had an incredibly busy term with an Ofsted inspection to contend with too. The inspection went very well and we have just received our report – which is very positive.

The team of inspectors were particularly impressed with all our procedures for eliminating poor behaviour and for raising pupil self-esteem.

In fact, the report cites the children's behaviour and attitudes in the school as very good! We also received a lot of praise for the quality of the relationships within our school.

At Blackwell, we all feel that much of our recent success can be attributed to the changes we have implemented re Circle Time and Golden Time, Lunchtime Golden Table and our Buddy System and Playground Improvement Project. Without the support and excellent training received via Jenny Mosley Consultancies, this would not have been possible. What we have implemented – based on your theories and practice – has literally transformed our school.

Thank you from us all

D Girdler

Del Girdler (Headteacher)

Blackwell Primary School achieved 'the most improved school in the country' status in 2002.

Why the colour gold?

Gold has been chosen for centuries to denote wealth and status. Just imagine – an adventurer's goal and an explorer's treasure. It conjures up pictures of the luxurious, exotic, gilt-edged plates at a feast; the cloth used for the finest clothes; the hero's reward; and the paintings on the palace walls.

> *As accurately as the colour sums up material riches, here we use the colour to indicate a richness of spirit, emotional wealth and the good things in life.*

Gold then, to us, symbolises a richness in positive values and qualities. As a society we find an enormous sense of worth in the skills of communication, giving, co-operation, understanding and sharing. Gold represents a psychological and emotional treasure chest that children can delve into, to support and encourage them through their learning and growing.

The Internet tells a golden story

Any search on the Internet for a topic will retrieve all manner of reading material – the good, the bad and the ugly. When 'Golden Time' was researched in this way, we found the odd article on golden retrievers and various golden times in history. We also found hundreds of references to Golden Time as used in schools' behaviour policies (see Chapter 11 for some golden examples). This in itself is a huge tribute to the esteem in which it is held by schools that use it.

Golden Time has been developed, tried and tested for you. We hope you enjoy this book and find the approach as useful as do the many who are already using and benefiting from it.

Behaviour and discipline

25. A new behaviour policy that has evolved through consultation has six Golden Rules and has incorporated an effective merit and sanction system operated by teaching and non-teaching staff. Pupils valued these incentives highly, in particular the use of privilege time or Golden Time, and staff, non-teaching staff and parents feel that the policy has made a positive impact on behaviour standards of achievement and the quality of learning.

Ofsted Inspection, June 1995,
Broadstone First School, Dorset

A golden class in a golden school

Classes and whole schools are termed 'Golden' when they all follow the Golden Rules and when Golden Time strategies are used to support the positive behaviour and relationships of all the children.

A Golden School is one where there is a feeling of emotional safety and where the values of caring and citizenship are at the heart of the curriculum.

The golden strategies in place help the children to listen to, and understand, each other. They are shown, through the positive modelling of the adults involved, how to build trust and engage in effective relationships. They learn how to make responsible decisions and wise choices through understanding that their behaviour has natural consequences.

As children take over ownership of their own behaviour and develop their inner locus of control (see Chapter 2, page 32), they become able to consider their rights, responsibilities and duties as individuals in a democratic community. When they take part in the process of formulating the policies that help run their school, they are effective citizens of that community.

> 71% of all our pupils wrote that one of the things that they enjoyed most about coming to our school was 'Golden Time'.
>
> *Ian Read, SENCo, Birley Spa Community Primary School, Sheffield (2002)*

The Golden School encourages the development of all the things in the following list:

empathy for others	good listening skills
respect for everyone	personal responsibility
a love of learning	staff having a sense of being a team
a democratic view	social skills and confidence
nurturing of pupils	decision making
making wise choices	confidence and self-esteem
positive relationships	communication skills
enjoyment of school	a safe environment
children having high aspirations	creativity
a wider sense of community	a wider sense of self
social inclusion for adults and children	positive social skills

Golden Time, used effectively, will help your school to become a school where these values are upheld.

To think about ...

◆ Golden Time is a whole-school celebration for the majority of children who have kept the Golden Rules.

◆ Golden Time is a positive behaviour-management system in its own right.

◆ This book gives a detailed explanation of what Golden Time is and how to use it.

◆ We use the colour gold to symbolise richness of positive values and qualities.

◆ A Golden Class or Golden School is a class or school that follows the Golden Rules and celebrates Golden Time on a weekly basis.

② What exactly is Golden Time?

Golden Time is a whole-school community celebration, a special reward session for the children who have kept all week a set of school values that we call the Golden Rules. Up to an hour can be set aside, during which every child is expected to stop work and have a weekly session in which very special, enjoyable activities are on offer. Children in early years or special school settings, and children who have low levels of inner locus of control (see page 32), would have a short daily session. With Golden Time to look forward to, children walk in on a Monday morning 'shining with gold' because the whole school trusts them to keep the Golden Rules! It is not a weekly earning strategy – it is a weekly 'I trust you to keep the rules' strategy.

What are the Golden Rules?

The Golden Rules are the means by which certain values are extended into every area of school life. They are a way of bringing concepts of morality and responsibility into the forefront of children's minds, enabling them to become more aware of their choices.

All members of a school are initially involved in the discussion and establishment of the Golden Rules. We have been involved in this 'drawing-out' process many times. We can honestly say that, never mind how many children in the school we consult, or the type of school, the children's ideas always fall into six areas of concern: to look after people physically, to care for people's emotions, to be the best you can be at work, to respect things, to respect people by listening to them, and to be honest. It is essential that you distil these concerns, which are often voiced in many different sentences, into simple, clear language that can be used by all children, parents and staff.

Consequently, the Golden Rules we advocate are the following ones.

We are gentle	We don't hurt others
We are kind and helpful	We don't hurt anybody's feelings
We listen	We don't interrupt
We are honest	We don't cover up the truth
We work hard	We don't waste our own or others' time
We look after property	We don't waste or damage things

Posters displaying the Golden Rules can be obtained from LDA. You can make your own photocopied version of our Golden Rules (see Appendix 1, page 147).

Golden Rules are moral values – not routines

It is important to remind ourselves here that the Golden Rules are an encapsulation of the deeper moral values, and are not the same as classroom rules, corridor rules, playground rules or dining-hall rules. All these sets of rules portray important boundaries for the children in different ways, and should be promoted alongside the Golden Rules (see Chapter 3).

Golden Time in a nutshell

 Children need a calm, safe ethos, in order to learn.

Golden Time is often held in the classroom or in special Golden Clubs elsewhere in the school. Sessions last up to an hour, and are usually timetabled to take place once a week. For early-years children, Golden Time may last for ten minutes every day, with an additional weekly special golden event being held with older pupils. Many schools choose Friday afternoons to coincide with the natural wind-down. However, schools with a high incidence of disruptive problems are encouraged to give Golden Time a high profile by choosing, for example, a Wednesday morning slot.

Many reward systems used to focus in a blinkered way upon children whose behaviour was often poor but showed improvement, or upon re-rewarding children who had achieved high levels of academic success. We believe these systems missed a crucial point, that the middle-plodder children who are regularly demonstrating thoughtful and responsible behaviour should be celebrated weekly.

> **We should celebrate the 'ordinary' middle-plodder child – they create the ethos and reputation of your school.**

Golden Time is a huge success as they strive hard not to lose it and appreciate the rewards for keeping the Golden Rules . . .

– behaviour improves across the board
– it provides the opportunity to have positive time with the children without pressure
– the records of loss of Golden Time kept by teaching staff can be used to support pleas for additional help with children who have lost their way

Una Gillespie, Headteacher, Cramond School, Edinburgh

Golden Time as a whole-school incentives and sanctions system

Used properly, Golden Time is a consistent reward system that is structured to reinforce the Golden Rules. Stickers, certificates and smiley faces are given to those who observe the rules. They are given by the whole school community – including mid-day supervisors, caretakers and children – so that people can all congratulate each other. This shows that all members of a community are entitled to respect and to be valued for their contribution. The celebration of success is built into Circle Time meetings, where verbal congratulation and class-team honours – certificates signed by all the class to each other – are offered.

The reverse side of these incentives is their withdrawal, which provides a sanction for breaking Golden Rules. This acts as a major encouragement to children to keep the Golden Rules in mind. Children who are always well behaved are rewarded, and the idea of fun is bound up in the whole policy.

IT WAS A GOLDEN DAY FOR ROSIE.

We need to celebrate the majority of children who adhere to the Golden Rules every day.

Sometimes, the middle-achieving majority of children in our schools could be entirely forgiven for:

- believing that poor behaviour and high academic achievement are the only types of behaviour that adults think deserve attention and recognition (negative attention being better than none at all);

- becoming encouraged to attempt misbehaviour themselves to gain attention;

- becoming completely disheartened if their academic work does not measure up to reward status and less inclined to have a go next time;

- believing that they do not deserve encouragement and reward for their continual valid efforts and day-to-day achievements.

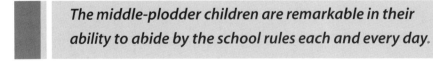

The middle-plodder children are remarkable in their ability to abide by the school rules each and every day.

Using Golden Time as a reward for keeping to the Golden Rules, the middle-achieving child, who can be relied upon to behave well and try hard, receives much-needed encouragement and acknowledgement. Their achievements are equally as valid as those of the child who misbehaves.

In awarding Golden Time to the whole class, the teacher can be secure in the knowledge that the children have received their just entitlement and is relieved of the burden of keeping a list of the rewards she has given to each child.

The psychology behind Golden Time

How are you to avoid letting your sanctions become a reward for attention-seeking children?

Currently, many schools are using sanctions as a reward. In the absence of a comprehensive reward system, sanctions are being handed out. For children who have an emotional hunger for attention, no matter how it is achieved, this is as close to a reward as they get. Key current sanctions range from detentions and lines to hanging out in an unofficial corridor club or missing playtime. We have seen children deliberately kick a child in the playground in order to be sent inside. Inside is warmer, and with a bit of luck they might end up having a chat with a teaching assistant. If you get children to write lines, you are using words as a punishment and those children are unlikely to become poets or authors. Shouting at a child increases their hunger for negative interactions and feeds their addiction to failure as a means of getting noticed.

In trying to address problems in these ways, nothing is being done to boost the child's self-esteem or to reward the other children, who have patiently obeyed all the Golden Rules. The fundamental concern is the children's emotional health. Focusing upon rewarding children's good behaviour will do more for the general mental health of the class (and that of the teacher) than relying heavily upon a sanctions system that is designed for specific children. It is a much more positive way of operating, and it will have a positive knock-on effect within the class.

Children's mental health is crucial to their academic and social learning and to their future whole health as adults. Many of the scenarios that society asks children to cope with – for example, extended or absent families, unbalanced diets, a polluted environment, an overload of advertising and television, hours spent amusing themselves on the computer, coping with friends or family in a chaotic state – can take their toll on a child's ability to develop in a mentally healthy and balanced way.

Children who are mentally healthy have been defined as having the ability to:

o   develop psychologically, emotionally, intellectually and spiritually;

➔

o initiate, develop and sustain mutually satisfying personal relationships;

o use and enjoy solitude;

o become aware of others and empathise with them;

o play and learn;

o develop a sense of right and wrong; and

o resolve (face) problems and setbacks and learn from them.

DfEE, Promoting Children's Mental Health within
Early Years and School Settings (2001)

Children need opportunities to practise and experience situations that allow them to explore all the avenues identified above. Working within groups and pairs; personal, social and health education (PSHE) sessions; and other activities provide some opportunities for practice within the classroom. Using the Golden Rule – Golden Time partnership can enhance these and provide a new framework within which to work with the children.

Maslow (1968) outlines how we all have basic and more advanced needs in life, and explains that we usually need and want more than we already have. In his hierarchy of needs, he describes five levels:

- physiological needs;
- safety needs;
- love and belonging needs;
- esteem needs;
- self-actualisation needs.

When the children have secured their physiological, physical and emotional safety needs, they need next to feel secure, and to know that they are loved and that they belong. After these comes self-esteem. Many children need a secure framework within which to work: to have a positive image of themselves and to receive recognition, attention and appreciation from others. This plays an important part in their learning. With the Golden Rules to guide them, receiving a regular incentive like Golden Time will help children to feel recognised for what they are achieving. The whole ethos of a Golden School and a Golden Class is that the children will feel special.

Encouraging a change in behaviour

As Key Stage 2 Co-ordinator I kept a week-by-week record of pupils who had lost Golden Time and so was aware of any pupil who was consistently losing large chunks of Golden Time. One Year 5 pupil in particular was regularly losing half or more of his weekly thirty minutes of Golden Time. I began to ask him during my playground duty if he had lost any Golden Time and what he had lost it for, and I talked to him about how he could gain it back. I started asking him, just in passing, at other times around the school too. It only took a moment. A change began to happen. It became more common for this pupil not to have lost any Golden Time and when he had he seemed to be more motivated to earn it back. I'm sure the conversations we had every week helped to instigate a change in his behaviour.

Jenny Huscroft, Class Teacher and Key Stage 2 Co-ordinator,
Birley Spa Community Primary School, Sheffield

Can Golden Time boost emotional intelligence?

In the last few years a very bright spotlight has been shining upon emotional intelligence, emotional literacy and issues surrounding self-esteem.

Daniel Goleman (1996) offers an alternative view to the commonly understood principle that IQ is a matter of intelligence that can be measured using academic-style challenges. He introduces the idea of a different type of intelligence, that of emotional intelligence, stating that this encompasses self-awareness, impulse control, persistence, zeal, motivation, empathy and social deftness. Peter Sharp (2001) defined emotional literacy as the 'ability to recognise, understand, handle, and appropriately express emotions. Put more simply, it means using your emotions to help yourself and others succeed.'

It is clear from research that emotional intelligence can be nurtured and strengthened in all of us. Goleman describes how the emotional lessons learnt by a child actually 'sculpt' the brain's circuitry. This is why a child's boundaries are so important. They provide a space for the child within which they can grow emotionally, in safety. Having rules is an important part of creating the boundaries for children to learn within. They need to understand why the rules are there and appreciate that they are meaningful. The Golden Time celebration of keeping the

Golden Rules reinforces children's perception of where the boundaries are, and their understanding that they are using the boundaries in the right way.

Attitudes, behaviour and personal development

37. Pupils are well behaved and courteous and aware that the school has high expectations of them. Pupils respond well to the 'Golden Rules' which provide clear guidance for purposeful and positive relationships with peers and adults. Clear definitions of appropriate behaviour and procedures enable pupils to take responsibility for their own actions.

Ofsted Inspection, July 1996,
Phoenix Secondary and Primary School, London

Inner locus of control

Golden Time can also assist in the development of the inner locus of control (ILC). Using one's ILC takes place when an individual assumes responsibility for their own actions and their consequences. They see themselves as being responsible for what happens. Using your outer locus of control (OLC) occurs when you blame other people for what happens to you.

To give some examples, a child using their OLC may say, 'I need some help because they keep winding me up.' A child using their ILC may say, 'I need some help because I lose my temper too quickly.'

The teacher using their OLC may say, 'If only we had better kids, you've no idea what a good school this would be.' Conversely, when using their ILC, they may say, 'I'm having a tough time; I need to get some help.'

Golden Time can help children move towards using their ILC. It gives a visual, tangible representation of the consequences of their actions. As we describe in later chapters (Chapters 3 and 5), having a warning card beside them, or having their name pegged onto a 'warning cloud', immediately displays to a very young child that they have a choice. They may choose to kick again, and they will lose a short privilege. ('What a poor choice, Sakira!') They may choose to stop kicking, and everyone celebrates together at Golden Time. ('What a great choice, Sakira!')

Social, emotional and behavioural education and our needs as individuals

The document *Developing Children's Social, Emotional and Behavioural Skills. A Whole-curriculum Approach* (DfES 2003a) was produced in recognition of the need to address these important areas within the scope of school activities. It outlines the fundamental importance of these skills. We foresee a need for schools to take an active lead in developing these areas and we believe that the Golden Rules and Golden Time partnership – especially when used within the context of a listening school (see page 85) – will provide those opportunities.

The SEBS programme

Social, emotional and behavioural skills (SEBS) underlie almost every aspect of school, home and community life, including effective learning and getting on with other people. They are fundamental to school improvement.

Various terms are used nationally and internationally to describe SEBS, including personal and social development, emotional literacy, emotional intelligence and social and emotional competence.

Where children have good skills in these areas, and are educated within an environment supportive to emotional health and well-being, they will be motivated to, and have skills to:

o Be effective and successful learners;

o Make and sustain friendships;

o Deal with and resolve conflict effectively and fairly;

o Solve problems with others or by themselves;

o Manage strong feelings such as frustration, anger and anxiety;

o Recover from setbacks and persist in the face of difficulties;

o Work and play cooperatively;

o Compete fairly and win and lose with dignity and respect for competitors;

DfES (2003a)

To think about …

Golden Time:

◆ is a time for all the community to celebrate the success of all the children;

◆ is when the most enjoyable, exciting and special activities are offered to children as a reward for keeping the Golden Rules;

◆ is a democratic system in which all children have an automatic right to the same privileges;

◆ is based on the assumption that all children will keep the Golden Rules;

◆ makes a contribution towards addressing self-esteem and emotional health issues within the classroom;

◆ offers opportunities to children moving towards using their ILC and becoming more responsible for their own actions and reactions, which is linked with building their self-esteem.

3

How to set up Golden Time

Starting things off

Golden Time can be timetabled as a daily or weekly session (depending upon the age of the children). Setting it up and building it up, and the importance it is given, can make a great deal of difference to its success. It is vital that time is spent paving the way before its introduction, so that it is fun and successful from day 1.

Please note that the following description of setting up Golden Time is aimed primarily at teachers of Key Stage 2 and older Key Stage 1 children. It would be helpful for practitioners teaching early years and children with special educational needs also to read this section, then to adapt it to suit different groups of children with reference to Chapter 5, where modifications are suggested.

It is of paramount importance that all the children and staff know why Golden Time is there – in other words, why you are bothering with it. Linking Golden Time with the Golden Rules and the school's behaviour management policy makes it effective. Some parents will wonder what this Golden Time is all about or why a child is sitting in front of a sand timer. It is vital to explain the policy to the parents as well as to the children.

> *Children who are used to gaining attention and status for misbehaviour need to see ordinary, rule-abiding behaviour receiving even greater celebration and acknowledgement from everyone.*

Many schools publish their behaviour-management policy in their school brochures, on their Internet sites or in parent information leaflets, explaining how it works within the school. Sometimes parents are asked to sign a parent–school partnership agreement which helps cement the ideas and the reasoning behind Golden Time (see Chapter 11 for details about explaining Golden Time to parents and carers).

Step 1 – setting the scene

Set up a discussion about the Golden Rules for all the teachers and children. As mentioned previously, these tend to fall into the following six categories:

① We are gentle – respect for physical safety.

② We are kind and helpful – respect for emotional safety.

③ We work hard – respect for work.

④ We look after property – respect for property.

⑤ We listen – respect for other people's views.

⑥ We are honest – respect for honesty.

Display the Golden Rules in several places in the school, surrounding them with photographs of children keeping them. We need to group the values with which we are concerned and call them the Golden Rules. However, not all children will access them via the written or spoken word. Some will need to see pictures of children keeping them. It is a fascinating exercise to sit with children at all key stages in Circle Time and ask them what photographs they would use to show children keeping the Golden Rules. For example, for the rule about being gentle, early-years children might choose a picture of a child playing gently – perhaps doing construction – and in Year 6 they might choose a picture of an older child looking after younger children.

Beware of confusing your Golden Rules with everyday routines.

Over the last eighteen years we have been to thousands of schools. One of the biggest problems that we come across is finding that moral values (the Golden Rules) have become muddled up with classroom routines. That means we see on the walls displays with messages such as 'We are kind and helpful, walk on the left-hand side of the corridor'.

Some of us are passionate about where the scissors go, but such detail is a preferred routine, not a moral value. Keeping children safe means that you must constantly negotiate with them regarding the safest routines to govern a particular area. We call the results of that negotiation the classroom, corridor or lunchtime rules. They are not the Golden Rules (the moral values), but they are equally important.

Every area of the school needs both sets of rules displayed, with photographs. Children learn best by choosing pictures of themselves keeping the rules.

Once the Golden Rules or moral values are established, they need to be constantly discussed and celebrated through assemblies, especially after every holiday. All the staff should be present. This can be done in Circle Time games and activities, and by using stories and poems that place the Golden Rules at the heart of the school.

In contrast, the class rules, playground rules, lunchtime rules and corridor rules need constant negotiation with the people who use them, including mid-day supervisors, cleaners and school caretakers. These rules should also be illustrated with photographs of children keeping them. Do keep changing the photographs to show different children; these displays should be an ongoing, vibrant part of school life.

The two sets of rules can be placed side by side on the wall; both are equal in relation to the Golden Time reward and sanction system.

To reinforce the importance of the rules about routine, a teacher might say, 'Do you know what corridor rule you are breaking now? No? You are breaking the one about getting into line calmly outside the door.'

Step 2 – deciding upon the golden activities

First, explain to the children that we have collected together all the class rules and the school has agreed upon the Golden Rules. Now find out what activities they would find so exciting and enjoyable that they would represent a huge celebration of the fact that they have kept all the rules all week. Brainstorm the choices with the children and decide what you can put up with in the classroom. Ensure that you include board games – these are the key to behaviour management. Good old Snakes and Ladders helps children learn to abide by rules, wait their turn, accept that life is unpredictable and arbitrary, and learn the anger management technique of showing nothing in their face – if they show bad temper because they lost, their peers will not allow them the chance to try again.

> When we started Golden Time we had a large display which I organised with photographs and activities listed. A clipboard was sent to each class at the end and the beginning of each week, firstly to find out which activities were being organised and then which activities pupils wanted to participate in. Pupil names were displayed below the activities. This has now evolved so that some classes work on their own during Golden Time and some work together, but all staff help each other with different activities.
>
> *Aileen Ronald, Headteacher, Allanton Primary School, Shotts*

Choosing Golden Time activities

In some ways, choosing Golden Time activities is the most important thread throughout your Golden Time preparations. The wish to carry out those exciting activities drives and motivates children to abide by the Golden Rules and makes them want to participate fully in the Golden Time celebrations.

With most children, it does not take long to find out what activities they find motivating. During Circle Time, or in a spare five minutes, brainstorm the children on the activities they would choose to do. These can be displayed in a list or table. Each week the children choose what they would like to do. A photocopiable example is supplied in Appendix 1 (page 148). Activities can be rotated to change with the seasons or with the children's developing taste for particular activities. If one activity is very popular, make it available on a rota system.

On page 39 is an inexhaustible list of ideas, many of which came from children themselves. Fortunately, many of them link in with at least one area of the curriculum.

Clay or plasticine modelling	Crafts	Visiting adults coming in to lead sessions
Topics	Making lunch registers	Watching DVDs
Educational games	Making place mats	Cricket
Playmobil	Reading comics	Rounders
Music trolley	Collage	Netball
Puppets	Model making	Football
Art	Making books	Apparatus
Construction toys	Cooking	Binka
Computing	Planting seeds	Parachute games
Story corner	Making egg and cress heads	Disco
Garage	Jigsaws	Tie dyeing
Juggling	Board games	Bingo
Making masks	Sand and water trays	Bubbles
Dressing up	Making wings	A cup of tea in the staffroom
Small world play	Dog dressing/grooming	Knitting
Dog walking	Welly walks	Picnic
Making playground items	Colouring	Making equipment for lessons
Making an office writing centre	Weaving	Team games
Colour chalking in the playground	Willow sculptures	Country dancing
A reading corner	Paper shredding	Rhythm sticks
Line dancing	Paper folding	
Sewing	Story-telling sessions	
	Play-Doh®	

How to make the most of Golden Time

○ Each year we dedicate a sum of money to top up our Golden Time resources to ensure it is fresh and interesting for our children.

Aileen Ronald, Headteacher, Allanton Primary School, Shotts

Once you have put your energy into setting up Golden Time with your class, there are important points to bear in mind in order to help it remain a success for your children. The list on page 40 may help you to remember the main points.

Key questions for making the most of Golden Time

- ❍ Do I use only the best, most desirable games or activities?
- ❍ Do I vary activities regularly to include individual, paired or group activities?
- ❍ When we need more room for certain activities, do I use other spaces in the school – like the playground, hall, music room or computer room?
- ❍ For team spirit, have I tried to arrange some whole-class activities like parachute games or clapping games?
- ❍ Have I made everything to do with Golden Time really exciting and enjoyable, thereby providing a real incentive?
- ❍ Do I regularly review the activities on offer and consult with the children during Circle Time?
- ❍ Do I keep on introducing new activities to make Golden Time fresh and stimulating?
- ❍ Have I considered enhancing the occasion by decorating the room or area with gold-coloured banners, posters, curtains or wall-hangings to emphasise the brilliance of the event?
- ❍ Do I talk about Golden Time with enthusiasm and anticipation?
- ❍ Have I invited older people, like parents and grandparents, in to make it a real community celebration?

Step 3 – reinforcing the Golden Rules with discussion and action

The ability to keep the Golden Rules is the essence of Golden Time. Create about six warning cards for your classroom and laminate them (see Appendix 1, page 149). They are to be used as a prompt for a child who is breaking a Golden Rule and has already had a reminder.

Yellow card is the best choice to photocopy onto. Some teachers keep them in clear plastic pockets along with a list of those they have been issued to, so that they can at a glance remind themselves that they have given out a warning card to someone in the class. You could use a warning card if you have already given a child a warning look (that one with the flared nostrils and the protruding steely eyes) or a whisper. Simply place it

quietly beside the child. Sometimes you will need to have a whispered dialogue with them about which Golden Rule, or other rule, they might be breaking. Often they will know immediately and you will just place the card by them. They will then know that if they continue to break that rule while the warning card is out, they will lose five minutes of Golden Time. In the case of an early-years child, they lose one minute of Golden Time (see Chapter 5).

Do not leave any warning cards out all morning or afternoon. For the middle-achieving children, you could take the card away at break time, helping them to learn the value of delayed gratification. For a troubled child, hot with inner chaos, do not leave the warning symbol out for long. As soon as they stop breaking the rule, smile and put it back in its original place. The child's Golden Time remains intact. Using a warning card is a way of creating a bridge back to you – not a means of causing confrontation.

Be sure to display the procedure for Golden Time in the classroom with a large picture and a bubble enclosing, in bold letters, the message 'Behaviour is your choice'.

For the older child in Key Stage 1 or 2, the teacher should record any loss of Golden Time on a chart (see Appendix 1, page 150). This chart is kept in a drawer, not displayed. Do not delude yourself: children are always alert to justice and they will know exactly who has lost Golden Time and who has kept it.

Step 4 – losing Golden Time

When a child persistently breaks one or more of the Golden Rules and creates their own behaviour agenda, this brings difficulties and distractions, and wastes time for the whole class. The child will need to learn that there are consequences for their actions, and that the behavioural boundaries are there for a reason. This is an important life lesson which will help the child negotiate their way through growing up. In days gone by, the threat of all manner of punishments in school was often enough to keep us on the straight and narrow. In this new age, understanding more about the nature of motivation and self-esteem has helped us to realise that punishment may have helped to manage behaviour, but the withdrawal of a treat can be more motivational – especially in conjunction with the provision of an incentive. Children understand the fairness of losing Golden Time if someone breaks a Golden Rule.

Every class contains a few 'behaviour lemmings' – children who immediately want to jump over the edge, so they can lose all their Golden Time. Let us look closely at what prompts such unhappy and self-destructive behaviour. Some children have very low self-esteem and have become addicted to failure. Failure is safe as it stops the child having to hope or look forward to anything. Up to now, life has let them down. People have promised them things, then have not been there for them. Their attitude is, 'Here is a teacher promising exciting activities if I behave myself all week. I think I'm bad, and I don't like myself anyway. So what's the point? I would rather blow it all than look forward to something.'

We all know children who are behaviour lemmings. Some act like this because life is so chaotic at home that they cannot concentrate. They are hot and bothered and having a terrible week. Some children, not trusting their ability to receive positive attention, are addicted to being shouted at – it temporarily fuels false self-esteem. If you have a child who manages to lose all their Golden Time and it's only Monday afternoon, it may be for one of the deep psychological reasons above. Or it may be that your Golden Time is very boring – there is more joy in winding you up and watching you spiral around the classroom than there is in playing a board game with the dice missing or scribbling on old computer paper.

Do check with the child about how they are feeling in Bubble Time (your one-to-one chat time) and ask the question, 'What would make Golden Time better for you?' And do bring them back from the abyss of misery by offering them the chance to earn back some Golden Time. This applies only to children who have lost all of it. The most they could earn back is fifteen minutes (half of Golden Time), otherwise this opportunity would not be fair on the child who keeps Golden Time regularly but has lost five or ten minutes in a particular week (see Appendix 1, page 151).

Use your judgement regarding the earning back contract

If your behaviour lemming is joyfully running over to the cliff and jumping over the edge of reason, it may be because they have worked out that it is simply fun to blow the lot as they get the chance to earn some back. Therefore offer earning back contracts only at your own discretion. If you find you are offering them to the same child for three to four weeks running, then maybe this child is taking you for a ride. You will have to think about putting this child on a child 'beyond' strategy. To do this you would need to take your concerns about the child to a staff Circle Time and, if possible, involve the parents or carers (see Chapter 6).

How to use the earning back Golden Time contract

Ideally, the concept behind the earning back contract should be one of restorative justice. In other words, however the child broke the rule, they should repair it in the same way. If a child hurts another child by calling them unkind names, they could earn Golden Time back by thinking of the special qualities that the other child possesses. In Bubble Time, you could encourage them to think about the other child and later let them know what qualities they have thought about. If a child broke the work rule, then they would do extra work to make up for it. If they broke the property rule, they would help restore furniture or tidy the cloakroom. If it were any of the class rules, like lining up, that they failed to keep, they would have to demonstrate five clear examples of following that rule appropriately.

Restorative justice is a sophisticated system and needs to be worked on. In the first instance, it is enough to earn back Golden Time in any way that is convenient for the teacher. The earning back contracts are a more formal agreement; they have to be signed by both the teacher and the pupil after negotiation.

Lost Golden Time contracts

Although our school's policy for pupils who have lost Golden Time means that an agreement must be made with pupils on 'how they can earn it back', this was usually a verbal agreement, which was not always successful. However, a significant change happened when I started using the 'lost Golden Time contracts' from Jenny Mosley's photocopiable book.

I kept blank copies of these contracts readily available in class and taught my class that they needed to fill one in if they lost all their Golden Time during the week. I would often help them with the wording of the contract and then I would get them to sign it.

The act of the pupil filling in this contract and signing it was much more successful in helping pupils stick to the agreement and gain back their lost Golden Time. It proved much more successful in encouraging pupils to take responsibility for their own behaviour, rather than having it enforced by me.

(➡)

By the end of the year it was common, rather than rare, for all my class to have their full 30 minutes of Golden Time by the end of the week.

Liz Page, Class Teacher, Birley Spa Community Primary School, Sheffield

To recap:

- If a child loses all their Golden Time in the early weeks of the system being established, then they are initially eligible for an earning back contract.

- The child can apply for an earning back contact by having a sensible quiet chat with the teacher.

- They can earn back only up to fifteen minutes of Golden Time (half the session); it would be unfair on the children who occasionally lost Golden Time to let them earn back more.

- If the child persists in losing all the Golden Time, then earning some back, they may be playing the system.

- The teacher has the right to offer or withhold earning back contracts.

- The teacher will need to decide at what point they stop using the earning back system with the child, and consider whether to move to the child 'beyond' stage.

Step 5: when a child does lose Golden Time

Be sure to use a five-minute sand timer. Children with a high level of inner chaos have a poor sense of time. It is no good telling them to sit still for five minutes as they may panic, throw over their chair and walk out. A watch or a clock is indecipherable to a child who is hot with emotion. The beauty of a sand timer is that it calms children through visual means. By looking at the sand they can quantify how much time they have left. Watching the timer is almost hypnotic: you can't help looking at it because it's good to see that the sand is running through, representing the fact that you are nearer and nearer your chosen activity.

At the onset of Golden Time, any child who has lost time is directed to sit at a table away from the activity with a sand timer. The timer is turned the right number of times to mark the number of minutes lost. Once a child has completed their time out, they are invited to join in the activities.

It is essential for the child to have their metaphorical nose pressed against the window of opportunity they chose to kick in! In other words, a key strategy is to ensure that the child sits close to the activity they would have engaged in if they had not made a poor choice when the warning card was out. The sound of laughter, the chinking of dice and the flourishing of dressing-up clothes are all reminders of what they are missing. They also serve as signs of what they can return to if they sit calmly and watch their allotted time passing.

Losing and gaining Golden Time flow chart

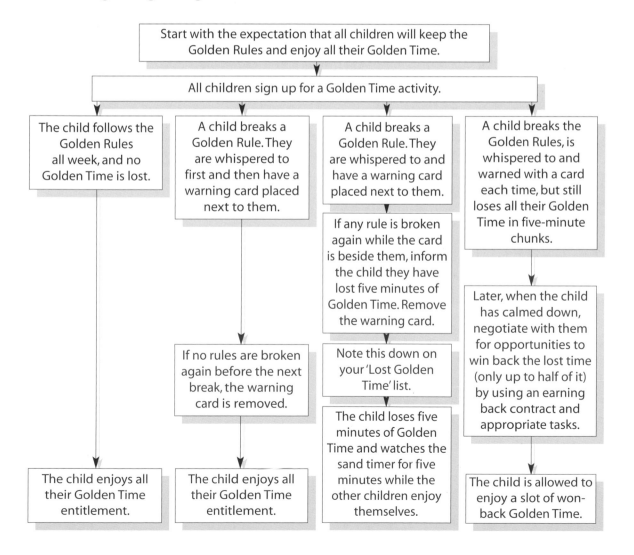

Start with the expectation that all children will keep the Golden Rules and enjoy all their Golden Time.

All children sign up for a Golden Time activity.

The child follows the Golden Rules all week, and no Golden Time is lost.

A child breaks a Golden Rule. They are whispered to first and then have a warning card placed next to them.

A child breaks a Golden Rule. They are whispered to and have a warning card placed next to them.

A child breaks the Golden Rules, is whispered to and warned with a card each time, but still loses all their Golden Time in five-minute chunks.

If any rule is broken again while the card is beside them, inform the child they have lost five minutes of Golden Time. Remove the warning card.

If no rules are broken again before the next break, the warning card is removed.

Note this down on your 'Lost Golden Time' list.

Later, when the child has calmed down, negotiate with them for opportunities to win back the lost time (only up to half of it) by using an earning back contract and appropriate tasks.

The child enjoys all their Golden Time entitlement.

The child enjoys all their Golden Time entitlement.

The child loses five minutes of Golden Time and watches the sand timer for five minutes while the other children enjoy themselves.

The child is allowed to enjoy a slot of won-back Golden Time.

Key questions to help you assess why children are losing Golden Time

If used wisely, loss of Golden Time is a very effective sanction, but lost Golden Time is not something that you want to see regularly. If a child or the whole class is losing Golden Time frequently, you need to reassess your approach. You could review the children's motivation in Circle Time. Consider the following questions:

- Have I made sure that the children understand the wording of the Golden Rules, the purpose of each rule and the hierarchy of strategies and sanctions?

- Have I made it clear that Golden Time is a celebration for keeping the Golden Rules and other rules?

- Am I using warnings too readily?

- Have I let Golden Time become boring?

- Do I continue to try earlier preventive strategies (whisper in time, reviewing, etc.)?

- Do I need to rethink a particular child's targets or my approach to that child?

- Have I given the child a verbal and/or visual warning, and do they understand why they have lost Golden Time?

- Am I leaving the warning out for too long or too short a time?

- Do I use my professional judgement about whether a child is moving towards their inner locus of control?

- Have I ensured that the child had sufficient time to respond to the warning?

- Have I provided plenty of opportunities for the child to earn back the Golden Time that they have lost, and are they fully aware that they have this opportunity?

- Have I made it clear that I want everyone to join in and enjoy the celebration?

- Could I foster a more positive approach amongst the children, in which they help one another to earn back Golden Time, working out an action plan (written or verbal) with the child to avoid future losses?

- Could I use being the first to sign up for the Golden Time activity of their choice with a friend on Monday morning as an additional incentive to their keeping the rules throughout the week?

○ Should I consider any additional issues that need to be addressed – such as moving the child to a different seat, tiredness, hunger, thirst, relationship problems at home or school?

Lost Golden Time

Waiting and waiting
The sand is sinking
All you can do
Is keep on thinking
As I wait
I start to mime
But if I get caught
I'll lose more time

Boy, aged 11
St Timothy's School, Coatbridge, Scotland

Step 6: rewarding all children

We need to praise to the skies the child who keeps the Golden Rules all day, all term. They probably represent at least 85 per cent of your class. They are a miracle. We have therefore designed some Golden Time Certificates that have to be sent home to their parents and carers through the post to give them high status. The certificates are a reminder of the value you attach to the Golden Rules (see Appendix 1, page 152). They are awarded to all the children who have

heeded their warnings (there is no record of the warnings) as well as those who have had no warnings. The child who has lost Golden Time may well have had extra motivation through the usual incentives – like stickers or smiley faces – to encourage them, but they will not receive the Golden Time Certificate. They can try for one next term.

A salutory true story

I was once working with a Year 6 class that had become 'high' on their own power. The NQT, anxious and nervous, had gone off sick; supply teachers had refused to cover; and their own power to frighten adults scared them. I told them I had been called in to help set up a positive behaviour system through Golden Time. A small core virtually said, 'Stuff your Golden Time, we're not interested.' I asked them what they were interested in, and they said, 'Football.' Now football is not usually in my scheme of things. I prefer to set up activities within the class as a way of getting children and teacher to enjoy each other's company. I like that to happen in the class because teachers can choose to ask 'difficult' pupils if they will teach them how to play a game and thereby recover the lost relationship. However, I am pragmatic. My learning from being in hundreds of schools is that initially the school must do whatever it takes to promote good behaviour. If football – or skateboarding – is the key to unlocking motivation, that is what we must do. We recruited a paid play worker to come in and do football during Golden Time for all the children from the different classes who wanted to play. Outside in the playground there was an empty table with the sand timer in the middle and a few children on chairs with very glum expressions round it – one eye on the sand timer and one eye on the exciting game.

It is a key strategy and I have known schools get it very wrong. For example, some schools set up Golden Time clubs so that children can choose a club for the afternoon. Several schools that did this reported Golden Time was not working. When I went to the schools to look, I found that they were sending children who lost Golden Time to a supervised quiet room where the sand timer was kept. This had become the Sin Club. Children seeking notoriety and kudos had to be seen to go to the Sin Club. What they should have done was put a table for those who had lost Golden Time in each of the clubs so that they could almost taste, smell and feel what they were missing as a result of their poor choice.

Jenny Mosley

If a child will not watch the sand timer

Motivation is the key to positive behaviour. If you have, through one-to-one chat time, talked to a child about how to make Golden Time better for them, but they still create a disturbance, you may well have to conclude that this is a child 'beyond' Golden Time. (Check first that what is happening is not a temporary aberration, in which case you can start the timer again and give them a second chance.) Similarly, if another child repeatedly loses Golden Time during the week, refuses to earn it back, and is then unable to sit still at the sand timer, you may decide that they too are 'beyond' Golden Time.

What this means is that the child is unable – because of social, emotional and behavioural difficulties – to keep the Golden Rules for six hours a day. In the child 'beyond' strategy, we totally reverse the psychology of the sand timer. We teach children to sit in front of a sand timer for one minute, keeping all the Golden Rules at once. This is one of what we call Tiny Achievable Tickable Targets (TATTs). By progressing from one minute to five minutes and then to ten minutes, you may be able to bring a child back within the scope of normal class behaviour. See Chapter 6 for more about the child 'beyond'. In Appendix 1 there is a photocopiable description of the procedure, and a target sheet you can use (see pages 156–157).

When to by-pass Golden Time

If a child engages in a physical attack or a serious verbal attack, having passed the warning card stage, they lose ten minutes' Golden Time instead of the usual five. This will be seen as fair by the other children. Serious incidents such as these mean that the child is reported to the headteacher, and the incident is written up in an incident book and read back to the child. This is then signed by all those concerned. There is an implication that parents or carers will be involved at some stage.

We have learnt the wisdom of recommending to schools that at the end of term they should rip up the incident book in assembly to symbolise the starting of a clean slate next term, even though some of the key information may have to go on another report for reference.

> My son hated having a particular incident held over him for years (it happened in a secondary school and was handed on from year head to year head in his personal file).
>
> *Parent*

Points to remember for setting up Golden Time

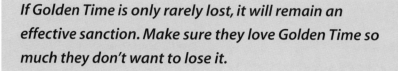

> *If Golden Time is only rarely lost, it will remain an effective sanction. Make sure they love Golden Time so much they don't want to lose it.*

There are a number of points to remember. The most important initial action is to talk to people and inform them of what you are doing – your staff if you are a headteacher, your headteacher and colleagues if you are a class teacher; other teachers; and finally the children and their parents or carers. Any concerns can be addressed at an early stage. You may find another teacher you can pilot it with, ideally so that younger and older children can work together in Golden Time.

Key questions for setting up Golden Time

- Have I introduced the Golden Rules to the class, linking them with Golden Time?
  Introduce and discuss the Golden Rules in Circle Time, illustrating them with a poster on the wall surrounded by photographs of children keeping them. Explain that keeping Golden Rules saves everyone much time and you would like to give them back that time to celebrate in Golden Time.

- Have I timetabled Golden Time?
  Timetable it and let everyone know – half an hour on a Friday afternoon is ideal.

- Have I made a reusable activities list?
  Prepare a laminated, wipe-off activity list with photographs of the activities being enjoyed. On Monday morning the children sign their names on it to do various activities. Since some activities will be especially popular, let them take turns to sign first.

- Have I thought about the activities and discussed them in a circle?
  Ensure you have quality activities for the children and vary them half-termly.
  In Circle Time ask the children each to name one thing that would make Golden Time better.

- Have I decorated and prepared the classroom?
  Materials or posters enhance Golden Time. Put these up at the beginning of the weekly session to mark the celebration.

- Have I let the children get a taste for Golden Time activities?
  At the first Golden Time, let all the children join in so that they can enjoy it and have an experience to relate to, irrespective of whether they have kept the rules. Make it different; make it fun!

- Do I remind them regularly about the Golden Rules and Golden Time?
  Continue to talk to your class regularly to make sure they know that you believe they are all capable of keeping the Golden Rules. Have practices at keeping them.

- Do I vary the activities and keep them fresh?
  If you have the energy, plan one or two whole-class activities or group activities for each half-term to keep the time special.

- Have I made sure that the children understand the whole system?
  The children need to understand the sanction of losing Golden Time and how to gain it back. And they need to know that this system is followed every day in a firm but fair way.

- Do I reinforce the rules in different ways – through Circle Times, assemblies, posters and photographs of children keeping them, displayed next to the rules poster?
  This addresses different ways of learning, as well as reinforcing the rules.

Do your best to let all children enjoy at least some Golden Time every week by providing the opportunity for them to earn back some lost time.

HM Inspectors found . . . most primary schools gave PSD appropriate emphasis in the curriculum. Many ensured that time was given to circle time, when pupils were encouraged to address sensitive issues; and to class discussions and/or Golden Time, when pupils were able to choose their own rewards for working well. Pupils often reported on this with enthusiasm and were clear about their purpose.

HMIE, Personal Support for Pupils in Scottish Schools (2004)

Day-to-day incentives that run smoothly alongside Golden Time

Golden Time flourishes within a culture of positivity and celebration. Children respond well to praise and encouragement, and there are many different ways in which children can be quietly encouraged during the day. Whilst Golden Time is at the heart of your incentives scheme, it goes hand in hand with day-to-day rewards and incentives. It is essential to create a positive culture and let every child know the taste of success. Within this culture Golden Time will flourish.

The following are ways of doing this:

- Thank children regularly for working or behaving well.
- Give out commendations or stickers during and at the end of lessons.
- Give children physical signs – like a smile, thumbs up, or a gentle pat on the back.
- Ask them to show and explain good work to the rest of the class.
- Use a class Golden Good News Book to record praise.
- Give duties out within the classroom, with appropriate responsibility badges.
- Let children take good work to show to other members of staff.
- Send notes home to parents commending their child's work or achievement of a tiny target of good behaviour.
- Ask the class to give someone a clap.
- Create 'fun' certificates.
- Consider asking the headteacher to create a weekly award tea party.
- Put smiley faces on stickers, or draw them beside good work or on the board.
- Create a class team honours certificate. (See Appendix 1, page 153, for one you can photocopy.)
- Acknowledge that you are pleased to have someone in your lesson.

To think about …

◆ Set up Golden Time in a structured way so that both you and the children know what to expect.

◆ Explain very clearly that Golden Time is a celebration for keeping the rules, and tell the children how it will operate.

◆ Make sure it is an exciting opportunity that children will really want to participate in.

◆ Ensure that the children know what happens if they break a Golden Rule, and be firm but fair in your procedures.

◆ If you feel it is appropriate, give children the opportunity to earn back Golden Time (only if they have lost it all).

◆ Use a sand timer to measure lost Golden Time, and make sure that children can see and hear the activities they are missing while they are waiting.

◆ Keep the activities exciting by regularly reviewing and replacing outmoded activities or games with new, more desirable ones.

◆ Run your Golden Time strategy alongside more day-to-day encouragement, incentive and praise strategies.

4 Keeping it golden

At first

When you first introduce Golden Time, create a range of activities within your own classroom, ideally pairing up with another teacher so that some younger children and older children visit each other in their classrooms. Different happy faces in the room help children associate the class with relaxation and fun.

We have found in schools where older children are helping younger children or teaching them new games, that not only does this boost everyone's self-esteem, but it helps children to develop empathy. If you take time to get to know others, you are far less likely to run into them in the playground.

Golden Time clubs

Some schools that have been developing Golden Time since the late 1980s with us have been looking for further ways to expand the concept. Golden Clubs were the answer.

Many schools have decided to encourage a community spirit by asking people from their locality to celebrate with them all the children who keep the Golden Rules all week. A list of clubs has been drawn up, including events such as tea parties with older people, a sewing club including parents, a keep fit club run by mid-day supervisors, arts and craft clubs with teachers and pet keeping.

Juggling Club

Juggling was set up as a Golden Time activity on request by Year 6 pupils. Two boys in particular were very keen, and often arrived at the activity before the supervisor. They collected the equipment from the store and set it up so they were ready to start when the other pupils arrived.

As the weeks passed by, they made suggestions to improve the activity. Their first suggestion was that the last five minutes should be used to celebrate new skills and achievements, no matter how small.

They then suggested that certificates should be given for being able to juggle three balls ten times, catch a diablo or spin a plate. These were awarded in our celebration assembly. During the Golden Time sessions, the pupils helped each other and shared their skills with patience, giving each other encouragement and praise. At the end of the sessions the children organised themselves to return equipment and clear away.

It was a delight to watch these two boys grow as the year went on. I'm sure their increased confidence and enjoyment impacted on other areas of their learning during their final year at our school. We hope to invite them back later in the year to run some juggling workshops for us.

Pat Greasley, Learning Mentor,
Birley Spa Community Primary School, Sheffield

The challenge these clubs pose to children is that they involve the practice of delayed gratification over a relatively long period. For a Golden Time club to work, it often needs to have a half-term devoted to it. Some schools run a 'taster fair' on the first Friday of each half-term so children can sample the activity. Because a child may sign up for an activity that they stop enjoying, you will need an open games club that anyone can join at any point. Elsewhere in this book (see page 48) we have reminded you not to create a sin club inadvertently, in which children who have lost Golden Time or misbehaved in their chosen club fetch up.

Keeping Golden Time fresh and exciting

It is vital to maintain the quality and freshness of the activities on offer. Remember to discard old, incomplete or dirty games. Keep a look out for games or activities that do not interest the children and remove them. You could have a round in Circle Time on 'Golden Time would be better for me if . . .'.

Parents' associations are sometimes willing to donate money to go towards purchasing toys and equipment for Golden Time. Although it is time consuming to visit them, car boot sales, fetes, jumble sales and charity shops often are good sources of things to do. You may make some very worthwhile finds; unwanted birthday and Christmas presents often turn up in such places. You could enlist the help of a friend who enjoys bargain hunting.

It can be very effective to alternate whole-class activities with individual and paired activities to suit your own plans for the class. Some teachers organise whole-class sessions, such as parachute games, pirates and other treats.

Only through Circle Time can you get to the heart of what the children really want to do in Golden Time.

Using different areas of the school

It is a good idea to make the classroom the centre of Golden Time activities. This will help to foster a feeling of community and will give children the opportunity to enjoy each other's company through playing games together in a close environment. However, certain other places in the school may lend themselves to activities such as parachute games and other co-operative games.

The playground and hall are ideal for group activities and are not always in use throughout the school day. One of our special schools purchased a number of bicycles. Each class had a session in the playground using the bikes on a rota system. Sessions like these can be just as productive as classroom ones, and can be used for teaching road safety or other skills with a specialist instructor.

What works in one school may not work in another. Children at one school we contacted enjoyed a cup of tea in the staffroom during Golden Time. They were briefed to use their speaking and listening skills in order to enjoy their chatting more. In another school, the headteacher invited children into her office for a special headteacher's Golden Time tea party as a treat. She enjoyed talking to the children and getting to know them better. This proved to be a highly successful and enjoyable session for all concerned.

Golden Time trolley

Some schools have a special golden trolley with games and activities that come out only during Golden Time. The trolley is taken to the classes in a different order each week so that each class sometimes has first pick of the toys and games.

Helping with a younger class or visiting an older class

Some children receive an enormous boost from being able to work with a younger or older child. One class can be paired up with a younger class, with children from each moving to the other class. The older children can teach the younger children games or songs, or help them with work. Do not take it for granted that the older child will know what to do with the younger child or understand how to help them. It is a good idea to allow the older child an opportunity earlier in the week to work out something to do with the younger child – learning a clapping game or skipping game, perhaps, or choosing a book or some pictures. They will especially enjoy teaching a younger child a game or helping them with construction.

As with any new initiative, novelty value will keep Golden Time fresh and interesting for a little while. Only when it is maintained as an exciting and wonderful celebration will it keep its magic, and its effectiveness as an incentive.

> *Keeping Golden Time fresh and exciting will increase its magic and power. Don't let it rust up!*

Key questions to help you keep Golden Time golden

- ⊃ Have I made Golden Time an important part of the week on the timetable so children know that it is given priority?
- ⊃ Do I continue to reinforce the connection between the Golden Rules and Golden Time?
- ⊃ Do I talk about Golden Time with excitement, in language that maintains its celebratory status?
- ⊃ Have I replaced old or broken toys and equipment?
- ⊃ Have I provided an opportunity to discuss Golden Time during Circle Time and found out if the children's interests have changed, so that some activities need to be replaced by something more exciting?
- ⊃ Have I let the children become bored with the activities?

- Can I think of new, inspiring ways of having a Golden Time, trying some whole-class activities like parachute games, or inviting a special guest, or including a special pet, or having a picnic?

- Do I award all those children who have lost no Golden Time during a half-term a special Golden Certificate that they may keep?

- Do I enable older and younger children to work together?

- Have we, as a school, considered starting Golden Time clubs (where children choose a club for half a term) when Golden Time has become well established?

- Do I offer any children who are not enjoying their clubs the chance of an open games club?

Shooting status and self-esteem right to the roof beams!

We just have to let you know – not only do we now have Golden Time 'up and running', but we even have a Golden Room!

We have transformed a room with £500-worth of new activities of the children's choice, with golden stars, golden material, golden blinds – and even golden confetti adorning the carpet. It's brilliant. We have 'Good News' slips which are taken home, and deducting minutes of Golden Time has made our discipline policy simple, but much more effective – no Corridor Club, no hours spent in reprimand. The staff love it, the children love it and the parents love it.

I thought we had a reasonably positive atmosphere, but Golden Time has shot status and self-esteem right to the roof beams.

Yours sincerely

C Kirkham

Mrs C Kirkham
Headteacher, Stourfield First School, Bournemouth

Other golden strategies to keep Golden Time special

Golden Time certificates

Certificates can be really important to children. They can be taken home, put on the wall, and shown to relatives in ways that other rewards cannot. Every half-term a special certificate can be awarded to those children who have not lost any Golden Time during that period. This is a celebration of their ability to keep the Golden Rules. They can take this good news home to their families, and keep their certificates as a reminder for when things are not as easy. The certificates can be ordered from LDA, or you can make your own (see Appendix 1, page 152).

The Golden Cushion

The Golden Cushion is an invaluable aid for fidgety children. Although all children will eventually have a turn sitting on it, its real purpose is to help the child who has difficulty in sitting still and staying focused. It can be used on the carpet or placed on the child's chair when they are working. The cheapest way of providing a golden cushion is to buy an inexpensive one from the market and cover it in gold cloth. The more dramatically gold it looks, the more attention it will receive.

Explain to the children that having the cushion for part of a day is a real privilege as it is only offered to those who are trying hard.

Golden Coins in a chest

The Golden Coins incentive is valuable for changing the psychology of the class. Children often collude to encourage one of their members to behave inappropriately. The result can be distraction, causing the teacher's focus to drift away from other children in order to try to bring the distracted children back to the point. If this is occurring in your class, you need to make it worth the children's while to change their patterns of behaviour. Providing a whole-class incentive is one approach.

You will need a chest of coins. These can be in the form of a two-dimensional wall display (see Appendix 1, page 154) or three-dimensional objects. (The children can make gold coins using modelling clay and gold poster paint – this is a good Golden Time activity.)

Choose a class target such as good listening, good sitting or working well. Explain to the children that when you see the class keeping this target, you will tick a coin on the wall display or put a coin in the chest. When the chest is full, the children can have extra Golden Time. You could keep a record of Gold Coins issued, and award a class certificate at the end of each half-term (see Appendix 1, page 155).

Gold Dust notes

Gold Dust notes differ from some other incentives as they can be a school-wide way of praising children. All the adults in the school community have a pre-printed pad of notelets to write messages on. Here is an example.

> **GOLD DUST NOTE**
>
> I NOTICED THAT:
>
> Karl in Year 6 helped to tidy the PE kits in the cloakroom before school without being asked.
>
> **WELL DONE!**
>
> Signed   Mrs Smith

Any adults in the school can give praise to any child, even if they are not in their class. The Gold Dust notes are written out and posted into one of the Golden Post-boxes within the school.

Golden Post-box

A simple Golden Post-box can be constructed out of card or a large tube or tin, and covered in decorative gold paper or material. Some schools have one post-box for the whole school, whilst others prefer to install a post-box in each classroom. All the Gold Dust notes are posted in the box and every day, immediately after lunch, the post-box is opened and the Gold Dust notes are read out. The recipients of commendations are applauded and the notes are pasted into the class Golden Good News Book. This ritual can really lift the day and start the afternoon off on a good footing. You may, of course, decide on a different time to open the post-box.

Golden Good News Book

The Golden Good News Book is a large scrapbook, preferably with a gold cover and gold embellishments that make the book look really special. Each class may have their own. You can use cut-out speech bubbles for children to write in positive comments about others. Older children can write their own statements and read them to the class. For younger children, you can scribe what they say, and let them stick the comments in the book. Gold Dust notes can also be pasted in. You could include photographs of more challenging children, taken when they are working well.

The Golden Good News Book could be made available in the classroom for children to browse through. Use it as a morale booster with the whole class by calling children into a circle and reading items from the book. Invite the children to applaud the comments, thereby celebrating all the good things that happen in the class. This can have a very uplifting effect and improve the mood of the class.

Golden Raffle tickets

We have helped some schools introduce a system of using raffle tickets to give to children when they have made a 'good choice' in their behaviour. For example, a child might have chosen to sit well, to listen well, or to be kind or helpful. The child is given a raffle ticket with on it the words 'Well done! What a good choice in . . .' The other part of each ticket is placed in a tombola drum or other suitable receptacle.

During assembly a Golden Drum Roll announces that the Golden Raffle is about to be drawn. Three to six winning tickets are taken out and the children with the corresponding numbers receive either a prize or applause. You could invite a different guest each week to draw the winning tickets, perhaps a governor or a member of the local community.

The use of such a system as this is dependent upon a school's policy. However, it is an excellent, cheap incentive system that can be extended to all the mid-day supervisors, secretaries – everyone.

Golden Peace symbol

Children are fascinating. We have noticed that some children, often ones with low self-esteem, actually enjoy having the warning card beside them. It is almost as if it gives them a chance to bask in a little bit of colour in what sometimes seems to be a grey world. They do not want to lose Golden Time, but somehow they like the security of being noticed. Therefore, we developed the concept of a Golden Peace card. You can adapt it from one of the dove pictures in clipart – we recommend a dove in a golden sky with a rainbow over the top. Alternatively, you could get the child to paint a dove. We decided, with the class, that if individuals or the whole table were particularly calm and controlled, then we would highlight this excellent behaviour with a laminated peace picture. The problem was sorted. All the children with this option are now desperately trying to be the proud, if temporary, owners of the new symbol.

In order to retain its impact, the peace card should be given to the child or children only for as long as they are able to maintain concentration and stay focused on their work. Use your judgement for each child.

Golden Peace Table

The Golden Peace Table is used by children to practise their negotiating skills. When a dispute has arisen between two children, they can elect to sit at the table for a maximum of five minutes to try to resolve their conflict.

It is important that a sand timer is used, otherwise children can sit for ages talking through their solutions. They should report back later on whether their ideas have been useful. It is a good experience for them to bring their ideas together and summarise what happened.

If children have been able to resolve a dispute on their own, they should be heartily congratulated – and provided with a sticker if an appropriate one is available. These skills are very valuable for the children, and if they learn by themselves, that will save the teacher time and energy.

The Golden Peace symbol can be used again, this time being displayed on the table during negotiations to warn other children not to disturb those involved.

Silence is golden

Ironically, many children yearn to have a chance to work peacefully on their own. One day, through a Circle Time, children expressed this need. We agreed that we would have several stand-up signs reading 'Silence is Golden'. Any child who wanted peace to finish a project could ask to use this sign. Once it was in front of them, no child or teacher could interrupt.

Children love this, but allow them to use it for set time periods only. Teachers may use the same sign if they are doing something special – but they must have time limits too – you cannot leave it out all day!

Involve parents through a Golden Exhibition

It is very important that the parents and carers of your children understand the ethos informing a Golden School. It is a good idea to invite them in to a Golden Exhibition once a year. This is an opportunity to inform them of your behaviour policy and to explain how all the systems work together to support one another. It is also a venue to inform the parents of the value of Golden Time as a class celebration, and tell them about its link to the Golden Rules.

Displays of the children's products and activities during Golden Time can make a colourful and exciting exhibition. The exhibition could contain a demonstration of Circle Time by a group of children. Ask children to speak about what they have learnt during Golden Time; that is always well received. Then encourage the visitors to get into small circles and discuss any games they used to play and any favourite activities. A great memory-boosting chat session always ensues.

Golden Dining Table

Our Golden Table has evolved over the years with our pupil council, who represent all our pupils, developing new ideas to extend the children's enjoyment at the table.

We started by putting a special tablecloth on the table. Four pupils were chosen to sit at the table. They qualified for this if they had been kind and caring to others during breaks (in the morning and at lunchtimes). All the staff were able to choose pupils to sit at the table. A special invitation to sit at the Golden Dining Table was displayed, and pockets containing the children's names were put beside the display. The four pupils who were chosen may each choose a friend to sit with them at the table.

The next year, our pupil council introduced orange juice for those on the Golden Table, and later flowers. This year they organised a table mat competition with eight winners being chosen. Who knows what will happen at next year's council?

Aileen Ronald, Headteacher,
Allanton Primary School, Shotts

The Golden Dining Table gives an opportunity for a couple of children from each class to enjoy a treat in front of the other children each week. A Golden Table can be set up using anything golden or special that enhances the look of it. The child enjoys something special instead of the usual dining experience. You can make the occasion really special by giving out invitation and congratulations cards (see Appendix 1, pages 158 and 159).

One school gives responsibility for its Golden Table to the mid-day supervisors. They decide which children deserve a place on account of good behaviour at lunchtimes and put slips with their names on in a Golden Box.

A mid-day supervisor's view

This is a positive approach to controlling behaviour at lunchtime. The children try really hard to get their name on a slip and look forward to the chance of getting on to the Golden Table.

Friday lunchtime is an exciting time as both the children and the lunchtime staff look forward to opening the Golden Box to see who is in it!

Sandra Baxter, senior mid-day supervisor,
Blackwell Primary School, Derbyshire

Special Golden Assembly

Special assembly board

Wow! Each Special Assembly in Blackwell Primary School is worth waiting for and everyone feels the buzz. Afterwards anyone receiving a Headteacher Award can look forward to seeing their name and their achievement celebrated.

Elaine Hull, Teaching Assistant,
Blackwell Primary School, Derbyshire

Some schools celebrate their children's successes in a special Golden Assembly, which may be held once a week or once a month. During this positive and uplifting assembly, any special achievements can be celebrated – events include the awarding of certificates, the reading of pieces of special work and the demonstration of a newly learnt skill or a piece of art or craft. Favourite songs can be sung, or uplifting music can be played, to create a sense of occasion and enjoyment.

This is an ideal time to draw Golden Raffle tickets or Gold Dust notes from a drum, read out entries pasted in a Golden Good News Book, or to make any special announcement. Stories that illustrate keeping the Golden Rules may be read, or stories illustrating special qualities shown by people's actions.

To think about ...

◆ Your language and the status you personally give to Golden Time will help the children learn that this celebration is important to you.

◆ Use only special, sought-after games and activities.

◆ Vary the activities, and talk with the children during Circle Time about what you do, to ensure that what you are offering provides a real incentive for them.

◆ Enhance the whole concept by using other Golden Time-related ideas and props – like a Golden Dining Table, Golden Time certificates or a Golden Post-box.

◆ Use Golden Time as a real celebration time for all concerned. Involve the whole community if possible.

Golden Time in the early years and special school settings

Golden Time has been very successfully used with Nursery and Reception children. Young children quickly learn what the celebration is and how best to achieve it. It is as useful in special education as it is in the mainstream. Some practitioners would argue that the use of positive incentives plays an even more crucial role in such schools, where taking responsibility for your actions and their consequences is crucial to the child's emotional growth.

Adapting Golden Time for Nursery and Reception children

The key principle, using Golden Time as both the incentive and sanction system, still applies. The purpose is to help the children to move from blaming others to accepting that they are an agent of change themselves. However, for very young children and for children with learning difficulties or severe emotional and behavioural difficulties, Golden Time becomes a shorter, more frequent event, initially taking place on a daily basis if possible. Their inner locus of control (ILC) will not have developed. They will be unable to work on the principle of deferred gratification. So, you need to start where the child is – in other words, they may need Golden Time for ten minutes every day.

The system has to be even more visual and easy to relate to for it to be effective within these groups of children. The children will quickly link in to the idea of

Golden Time being a reward for following the Golden Rules and the school's other rules if it is displayed to them in a very bright and visual way.

> **Young children will access the Golden Rules and Golden Time partnership easily if it is displayed to them in very visual terms using colour and pictures.**

How to operate the system

We advocate the use of a large, visual display, as illustrated. When children were consulted about this picture, they were very clear that the sun must be much bigger and more visual than the cloud. Try to honour this request.

The system has four steps.

Step 1

- ◗ A large, bright yellow sun with a smiling, happy face is constructed out of card or wood. Use the illustration of the visual display to guide you in making this.

- ◗ The rays of the sun are yellow clothes pegs and the reverse side of each peg is painted grey.

- There is a peg for each child in the class. The name of each child is written on the front of their peg and, if possible, a photograph of the child's face is glued onto the sunny side of the peg too. The grey side simply has their name on it.

- The sun represents Golden Time, and it is happy because all the children on its rays are going to enjoy the celebration.

- The usual, default position for all the pegs is around the sun, with the sunny side of all pegs facing outwards.

- You also need a sun and a cloud, made out of card or wood as before, and a grey cloud with a sad face.

Step 2

- If a child is breaking a rule, the adult gently whispers to them or gives them a 'knowing' look.

- If the child fails to respond to the warning, their peg is removed from the sun and turned round, so that the grey side is showing, and placed on the sun and cloud. The child will now know that they are poised precariously between the happy sun and the sad cloud shown in the visual display.

- They should then be encouraged to 'do the right thing', so that their peg can be placed back on the smiling sun.

- You can draw a comparison from the peg on its own, reminding the child that they will be feeling left out if everyone else is enjoying Golden Time while they sit out and miss some of the fun.

- If no further rule is broken, put the peg back on the golden sun at the end of the teaching session – these children are not practising delayed longer-term gratification. If the same child is repeatedly on the warning cloud, it is a good idea to start keeping a record in case the child needs further support at a later stage. (See Chapter 6.)

Step 3

- If the child chooses to break another rule while their peg is on the warning cloud, their peg is placed on the sad cloud. This will mean losing one minute of Golden Time.

- The stages should be explained very carefully to young children, as many times as needed, so that they are fully aware of the reasons for moving their pegs.

- They will see that their actions have logical consequences, both positive and negative, and be aware that these consequences do not change.

Step 4

- When Golden Time takes place, any child with a grey peg on a cloud sits away from the activity area, maybe with a helper, while looking at the one-minute sand timer.

- The sand timer is used to show the child how long they must wait before being allowed to join in the activities. They must sit and watch the timer quietly. When it is finished they will be invited back in for the rest of Golden Time with a clap and a smile.

- All children will finish Golden Time together and the shared fun will become the memory – not the image of a child outside.

> *Remember that young children may be adjusting to the new rules of school and will be in need of lots of positive encouragement.*

Enjoying Golden Time in the early-years setting

At the beginning of Golden Time, a large golden sign is put up on the door to enhance the feeling of privilege. The sign might read: 'We're enjoying Golden Time'.

It is important to ensure that Golden Time is fun and creates a community feeling. All the staff and helpers should be included, and the activities should be sufficiently varied to maintain enjoyment and excitement. Loss of Golden Time can be used as an effective sanction only if it really is a privilege to be included in it. Golden Time activities may include special games, singing, dancing to music, playing games such as Simon Says, drama activities and so on. Party games, such as Musical Chairs and Pass the Parcel, are much loved. One lovely aspect of working with these children is that, because the Golden Time sign is up, they reckon that whatever takes place is 'golden'. 'Oooh, it's "golden singing",' they may say.

> *Children with hot, bothered and chaotic minds, and also very young children, cannot access the spoken or written word. They can access colourful pictures as meaningful symbols. A visual warning speaks volumes to these children.*

Golden Time in a special education setting

Motivating an autistic pupil

During Years 4, 5 and 6 I had an autistic pupil in my class who had a joint placement at our school and a special school. Initially she spent the last two days of each week in our school, but this increased to three days by Year 6. Her socialisation at our school was very successful.

I tried to develop close links with her teacher at the special school that she attended in the first part of the week, and this led to a number of joint visits and activities. We kept a shared weekly record to ensure continuity between our two schools.

We found that the single most motivating effect on the behaviour of this pupil was Golden Time, which she took part in on a Friday at our school. We were able to affect her behaviour positively, not just at our school but also at the special school.

Hilary Read, Class Teacher,
Birley Spa Community Primary School, Sheffield

Children with special educational needs may have reduced levels of self-esteem and confidence. To the children the expectation that they will keep to the rules can be a confidence-booster in its own right. The expectations placed upon these children in other areas of life may be particularly low, and they sense this. To say to the child, 'I trust in you to keep the Golden Rules and all the other rules and you will receive a reward for this that we are going to plan right now', may be the kindest expectation some children are given all day.

To think about ...

- ◆ Golden Time can be an invaluable resource for early-years and special education settings.

- ◆ This celebration or reward can help all children access the concept of your incentives system.

- ◆ The activities on offer must be appealing, safe, stimulating and manageable, and there must be something for everyone.

- ◆ A visual display using the sun and a cloud helps children to understand the concept that behaviour is a choice and gives them very clear signals about what is expected.

- ◆ Making strong links between the Golden Rules, and other school rules, and Golden Time very clearly and in different ways is important; make sure that the reason for Golden Time is understood as fully as possible.

- ◆ Using photographs of children keeping the rules and enjoying Golden Time activities provides a visual reminder of the system.

- ◆ Golden Time will need to happen more frequently if children find the concept of delayed gratification too hard to grasp.

- ◆ Any loss or earning back of Golden Time for non-adherence to a rule may need to be evaluated and adjusted for each child, depending upon their particular set of challenges.

6

The child 'beyond' Golden Time

Some background

When we go into schools, many teachers immediately insist that they have at least six or seven children in their classrooms 'beyond' Golden Time. To us, this statement often reveals that the practitioner has not yet put the entire system in place. We have worked in thousands of schools, improving the good ones and turning around those in special measures. Golden Time, if carried out properly, has never let us down. It has always worked for the majority of the class, and only a few children are really beyond its benign, all-embracing ethos. You would need to put your hand on your heart, look one of us directly in the eye and state that you had genuinely tried all the strategies for Golden Time laid out in this book before you could claim that a child was beyond it!

We coined the term 'child beyond', not to refer to a child as beyond help, but to a child who is beyond being able to respond to, or benefit from, the normal proactive motivational procedures used in the Golden Time incentives system. This is the child who has repeatedly been given opportunities and different modes of support in order to help them achieve levels of behaviour that are mostly acceptable, but has been unable to respond. See Mosley (1996 and 1998), *Quality Circle Time* and *More Quality Circle Time*.

We are happy to highlight here, briefly, extra strategies you can try with these children. However, our focus in this book is on how your school can meet the needs of the majority of children. The minority of children who are 'beyond' deserve and need specialist attention that is outside our present scope.

How our current strategies support inclusion

When it is agreed by you and the other adults that a child is beyond keeping the Golden Rules, and other school rules, for the six hours of a school day, there are strategies that can be used to support the child's inclusion within the class. Some of these involve reversing the psychology – from that of celebrating the child who keeps the rules all of the time, to celebrating when this particular child keeps a rule for a short time. That enables the child to be praised for an achievement.

When a child 'beyond' has lost Golden Time, and seems unable to sit for five minutes with the sand timer keeping the Golden Rules and other rules while waiting for Golden Time, you could use the sand timer to monitor a five-minute focus on the rules.

The child needs to agree to sit with you and target a behaviour they find difficult, such as sitting calmly on a chair, or focusing on work or a game. The sand timer is placed beside the child. If they cannot keep the rules for five minutes, then try three minutes – or two minutes or one minute. The key to the strategy's success is allowing the child to experience achievement and success. The child may well be frightened of their own behaviour. If they could trust in their own ability to self-regulate their behaviour, even for a few minutes, that would help them to gain the courage they need to face greater challenges. Children must be able to taste success. Failure is safe – success is terrifying as it leads them to think 'I might start to hope again, and maybe I am so bad I won't be able to do that good thing again.'

Children at this stage may need a series of different approaches that will not be appropriate for the rest of the class. This is because of their complex levels of inner chaos and distress. All children have the basic need and right to experience an enriching curriculum and positive teaching relationships. There are three other approaches that can be drawn upon, as detailed in the rest of this chapter.

Helping a child 'beyond' Golden Time

Behavioural management support
Tiny, achievable, tickable targets
supported by visual symbols

positive
relationships
+ enriching curriculum

Therapeutic help
Circles of support
Play therapy
Counselling

Peer support
Mainstream Circle Time
Playground buddies
Golden Time mentors

Behavioural management support

It is vital to give these children back a sense of self-worth, and to support them in taking back control of their own behaviour. One way of doing this is by providing a guaranteed success system, such as Tiny Achievable Tickable Targets (TATTs); see Appendix 1, pages 156 and 157, for a description of the procedure and a target sheet. The initial stage can last for two- or three-minute sessions in the morning, during which the child's target is an agreed standard of work or behaviour which is achievable. Once the child succeeds at that standard, it can be raised or the time period can be extended.

Therapeutic help

These children will benefit from opportunities to attend small therapeutic circles of support, where they will work with support co-workers. These circles can incorporate up to twelve children with a range of emotional needs. Ideally, two adults act as co-workers. At this stage parents and other agencies are brought in to contribute to the approaches being used by the school. In these circles, the child receives unconditional warmth and respect.

However, some children need one-to-one support. Art therapists or counsellors may be brought in for weekly sessions with them. Once children see troubled children being offered this sort of help, they come to see the school as a moral community prepared to support its more disadvantaged members.

Peer support

Self-esteem is often an important issue for these children. A reputation goes before the child into the next class, and it spreads throughout the school and to the home. People will look out for problems when this child is around. The child will see negativity reflected in the eyes of people wherever they go, and their poor self-image will encourage the child to become the difficult, problematic person they have come to believe that they are.

It is important to consider the wider implications of the child's behaviour. For example, what impact does it have on the rest of the class? Maybe it suits the class to help maintain this child's inappropriate behaviour – for entertainment, or to fulfil a personal agenda of feeling better about themselves. If the children can help to wind up a troubled child, or report a child who is misbehaving, they may succeed in getting someone else into trouble, in winding you up, in making any of their own shortcomings become overlooked, or they may achieve a number of different outcomes. If the class have a vested interest in this cycle of events, it is important to acknowledge this and to find a way to prevent it.

An excellent strategy is to consider making the child's daily target a class target. For example, the target could be sitting calmly in their seat. Class target wall charts can be used (these are available from LDA), or you can make your own. The procedure is that, with the prior permission of the troubled child, you get the class to agree in Circle Time to support the child. Their target becomes a whole-class target. You display an attractive target sheet poster with the target clearly written at the top – in this example 'We are all trying to sit calmly in our seats'. You explain that every time this child reaches their target they can contribute a star or fish to the poster (if using the LDA design), covering its white outline on the poster. The child will contribute the majority of the symbols. However, you would like everyone in the class to show that they can model this good behaviour too, reflecting the theory of social learning (Bandura, 1977).

During the day, you try to notice the required sitting behaviour of any of the children and celebrate their success by inviting them to put a symbol on the poster. Once the poster picture is complete, the whole class is given a social treat such as parachute time. In this way, the class learns that there is something to be gained from helping this child to be 'good' – that is, staying on task – as opposed to what happened on previous occasions, when there was much to be gained from helping them to be 'naughty'.

Helping a child to be 'good', as opposed to helping them to be 'naughty', can become a class target.

Key questions to consider when a child is 'beyond'

- Do I always remember to smile and welcome the child 'beyond' every day, thereby helping us both to start each day afresh?

- Could I start a TATTs system, with a peer mentor, to reward the child's efforts?

- Do I offer to help this child through Circle Time?

- Could I negotiate with the child quietly in Bubble Time (a one-to-one chat time) about behaviour I find it hard to tolerate?

- Have I considered organising a small therapeutic circle of support for children 'beyond'?

- Could I suggest the school operates a community taskforce at lunchtime to keep these children out of trouble?

- Do I know how to protect myself and my own feelings in these situations?

- Could I suggest we have a regular Circle Time for staff to discuss our concerns about individual children?

- Am I brave enough to ask for help myself, admitting that a child is seriously threatening both my and my class's emotional health?

- Could I suggest a timetable of support created by the staff to give the child and the rest of the class a break from their interaction?

- Am I prepared to occupy a troubled child in my class to give a colleague respite?

- Can I accept that it is not my colleague, my school or myself that has failed this child? It is this particular mainstream system that is failing the troubled child. These children need more limited boundaries and contacts to make life and work safer for them. Can I let go of any guilt I may feel concerning this child?

- Am I prepared to step up my personal care plan during this stressful period in order to look after and replenish my own energy?

Beyond the 'beyond'

If the child in question has not responded to the efforts and strategies of the teacher and the school, a serious stage has been reached. This is when, as a staff, you agree that the consistent application of the strategies already outlined has failed and that this particularly troubled and troubling child can no longer benefit from the mainstream provision your school is offering. At this stage the emphasis must shift from trying to support the child to include preserving the teacher's sanity, the sanity of your colleagues and the sanity of the rest of the class. The headteacher will also need support during the process of completing endless forms and lobbying the authorities to place the child into special education or to obtain support from them.

When you are expected to cope with challenging behaviour

When challenging behaviour strikes, there are many different actions and reactions we may have. Certain actions may help to improve the situation in some instances. It is necessary to involve parents or carers, although this involvement will vary according to how they perceive the child's behaviour. Much may depend upon previous interactions between the school and the responsible adults.

When we look objectively at this whole area, we see that it is not logical for a child to choose to behave inappropriately and fail to gain a reward when they could achieve a reward by behaving well. Everyone enjoys praise and the appreciation of others, but some children develop the habit of producing challenging behaviour and become addicted to failure and negativity. It is clear that their behaviour is a sign of distress.

You will need huge amounts of patience, as coping with challenging behaviour may be a very gradual process. Some children will need a long time to respond to your strategies, and some may respond minimally or not at all until after they have left your class. Don't expect the child to be transformed overnight. Even if they are aware of their inappropriate behaviour and know what they should be doing, old habits die hard. Sometimes the child may be really trying to change and may succeed for a while, then give in to their earlier behaviour. Support at this time of transition is of paramount importance, otherwise the child may become despairing and give up. Ensure that both you and the child have a realistic view of improvement and progress. Remember that events outside school will be affecting the child in various significant ways, and that it may be difficult for the child to achieve change at a particular time because the family is under pressure.

Be prepared to organise a personal visual timetable for a child if necessary, even if their routines are different from the other children's. Be aware that you may have to accept that certain children will always be different and will not conform fully. This is fine if the child's behaviour does not deter themselves or others from learning, or you from teaching effectively.

While you model the desired behaviour as an example to your class, remember that children will imitate the behaviour of role models who confirm their present behaviour. It is hard for children who have learnt inappropriate behaviour to learn correct behaviour from you. Moreover, even though a child may have a really positive, strong role model in their teacher, they may not adopt appropriate behaviour if the rewards are not as great as those they receive from inappropriate behaviour. The influence of a subgroup here may be more important and influential to them.

Whatever stage the child is at, your Golden Time strategies will be crucial. The key is to offer the child a tangible reward for positive behaviour.

Key questions to help in the face of challenging behaviour

- Have I got to know the child as best I can?
  Persevere with this; these individuals may be mistrusting of adults.

- Have I avoided the temptation of labelling the child as 'bad' or 'naughty'?
  This only reinforces a negative stereotype and the label may stick.

- Do I talk with the child and remain empathetic to their lives and problems?
  If a child thinks you are on their side, they will be more open to your approaches.

- Am I helping the child to learn new ways of fulfilling their need to gain attention?
  Children need to be shown behaviour that is as rewarding as less positive behaviour.

- If a child expresses anger inappropriately, have the class and I worked with them to learn to express it in a more appropriate way – like doing physical exercises, counting to 10 or clutching a stress ball?
  Constructive anger management will teach the child that there is another way to deal with these feelings.

- Do I make every effort to praise even the smallest improvement?
  Children with low self-esteem will need you to pick up on every opportunity to praise them and notice any small positive sign.

- Do I log inappropriate behaviour to discover what it achieves for the child?
  Does the child seek attention, avoid work or gain sensory or tangible rewards? (Motivation assessment scales from your educational psychology service will help you to determine this.)

- Do I avoid getting drawn into familiar and well-practised negative scripts?
  The child's role is to behave inappropriately and be reprimanded or sent out of the room or threatened with punishment. If you take part in this, you will reaffirm their view of themselves. Change the script – make it a positive one.

- Do I remember never to use force to try to coerce a child into doing something?
  It is unlawful, and will almost certainly escalate the situation.

- Are my body language and voice non-threatening?
  Avoid shouting, pointing, folding arms, placing hands on hips and waving hands or arms.

- Do I insist that a child looks at me?
  If they are already upset, this can make them even more uncomfortable.

- Do I use a reassuring touch with care?
  Know your child well before soothing through touch.

- Do I allow prejudices to lead me into making incorrect judgements?
  A child may not have meant to be cheeky; and a child may not be stubbornly refusing to answer you – perhaps they simply can't think what to say.

- Do I tend to take negative behaviour personally?
  The child has enough problems without having you feeling threatened to contend with. Stick with the behavioural issues and do not take things personally.

Remember to strike while the iron is cold

Emotional storms are not the way forward. There are certain actions and responses that are acknowledged to have a calming influence and help to defuse a situation.
Listen to a child's version of events and don't always assume the worst.

Key questions to help you keep the situation calm

- Do I talk to the child in a calm, even voice, redirecting or diverting them, where possible, to another activity?

- Do I give the children enough time to respond, and further opportunities to take responsibility for their behaviour?

- Do I talk to the child away from the rest of the class if they need a chat with me so that they do not lose face in front of their peers?

- Do I remember to postpone discussions until the child is feeling calmer and emotions are not running high?

- Do I always remember to treat inappropriate behaviour as an occasional unfortunate lapse on the child's part?

- Can I open my mind to the possibility that something could be done a different way, or that changing a system might be for the better?

Circle Time rituals for re-creating calm classrooms

Quality Circle Time can be used at times other than in scheduled Circle Time lessons. Sometimes the whole class seems unsettled. Rather than battling on regardless or handing out a blanket sanction, take a few minutes to try to settle and refocus the children.

Key questions to help you create Circle Time rituals

- When the children need calming, do I guide them to do breathing exercises?
  Inhale for the count of 4, then exhale for the count of 7. Repeat for a few minutes. This does have a physical response. Eye movements slow, facial muscles relax and the heart rate slows down. The head clears and the body's muscles relax.

- When the children are having trouble concentrating, do I play a couple of short games that require them to focus their thoughts?
  For example, Simon Says, in which you give the children instructions in quick succession.

- When the children need to regain their focus, could I try the following activity, called Switch?
  You perform an action such as tapping your head. The children do not copy until you call 'Switch'. At this point you change your action, but the children tap their heads. You continue to call and change the action. The children are always one action behind, so they need to pay attention to what you are doing.

- When the children need energising, could I perform a couple of co-ordination exercises to stimulate the whole brain?
  For instance, try clapping games with a song, or putting one hand on your nose, the other on the ear opposite to it, then swapping hands so the other hand is on your nose and the second one on your ear.

Explaining special treatment

By and large, children are very accepting of the special treatment that some pupils receive. Whilst they may not be able to verbalise the reasons for this, they have an innate understanding that the child in question is different and needy in some way.

Sometimes there are children in your class with conditions like Tourette Syndrome, ADHD, Down Syndrome and Asperger syndrome. The other children will realise that these pupils behave somewhat differently from the way in which they behave. The majority of children enjoy the experience of school and learning, and do not like to have their lessons disrupted or to witness behaviour that may be unsettling or even frightening. They therefore accept that some children need a different approach.

In these situations, it is best to make what is subliminally understood externally understood too. Before you do this, ask the permission of the child and their parents, and see whether they would like to enlist the help of the class. Ask the child if they would like to be present during the discussion, or whether they would prefer to be absent. If they choose the latter, have a debriefing chat with them later.

Explain to the children some of the strategies that you would like to try as a group. Whatever stage the child is at, their actions will be endorsed by the other children so that they can become part of the system. Tell them that certain children need larger slices of your attention cake than others. Other children deserve a slice of the cake too.

All the children should regularly receive a certificate to thank them for supporting each other.

When children do complain of unfair treatment – that inappropriate behaviour seems to result in rewards for one child and sanctions for the rest of the class – take time to discuss this with them. Remind them that all children are different, in height, weight, appearance, skills, and abilities. The children will know and accept this. Explain that they are also different in things such as ability to sit still on the carpet, ability to listen well, ability to focus on their work and so on. Most children are able to do these things easily. Children who find these things difficult will need a little leeway and extra encouragement to succeed. The special arrangements for them are a temporary aid to help them become more like the rest of the class.

Sam, who has Down Syndrome, shared Circle Time with his peers successfully from the start of his schooling. His classmates intuitively knew that he needed extra support and all, without exception, provided an environment within which he felt supported.

The importance of Circle Time was highlighted when Sam transferred to his junior school. His class was as supportive as ever, but problems arose in the playground. Some older boys who saw him as an 'easy target' singled him out. Excellent management by his class teacher ensured that these potential problems for Sam were 'nipped in the bud'.

The class teacher visited the offenders' class and Sam's special needs were talked through, during circle session. Time was set aside for the offending boys to work with Sam. A relationship was soon established and a negative experience soon became a positive one for Sam and the older boys!

Di Howells, Sam's proud mum

To think about …

- ◆ Recognise when a child is beyond using Golden Time as a strategy.
- ◆ We recommend these children are offered three levels of support:
  - − behavioural management support − working with adults to achieve TATTs (tiny, achievable, tickable targets);
  - − therapeutic help − circles working closely with adults in a fully supportive environment;
  - − peer support − consider the way the class interacts with the child and try to stop or change any negative cycles.
- ◆ Try to recognise when a child is beyond these measures and work as a staff team to manage the situation, so that the child receives appropriate measures and individual staff members are not left to deal with the situation alone.
- ◆ Use lower-level techniques to calm and communicate with a more disruptive pupil. These can go a long way towards creating a calmer and more productive atmosphere.
- ◆ Be aware that some children may not immediately understand or accept the special treatment of other children. Make sure that this does not become a further problem or work against your efforts with the child who requires special treatment. Take time to discuss this with the children, and try to enlist their support.

7

The place of Golden Time in the Quality Circle Time model

The need for a 'listening' model

The culture of change – change within families, communities, schools and nations – is with us to stay. We have to deal with that. Adults, on the whole, lead such busy lives that rarely do they have time to sit and listen to their children without being distracted. They do not often encourage children to explore their relationships in a calm and centred way. It is understandable that aspects of our society are becoming increasingly emotionally dysfunctional.

Children have always had a lot to cope with, and we expect children to deal with massive issues at the same time as they are learning about themselves and their world. It is remarkable that so many children do well with their own relationships and lives. Some do not fare as well. Many children need time in an emotionally safe place, with people whom they know and trust, to learn how to listen, respect other people and express how they feel. Quality Circle Time provides all this for children.

Quality Circle Time provides more than this. Adults need to be listened to as well. The system works by offering listening circles at all levels in the school, not only in the classroom. Just as the children will sit in a circle with the teacher, so the teacher will sit in a circle with other teachers, support assistants, mid-day supervisors and all other people who are working and contributing to the ethos or running of the school.

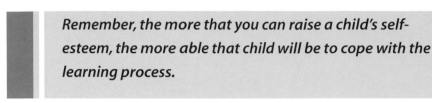

Remember, the more that you can raise a child's self-esteem, the more able that child will be to cope with the learning process.

Where did Golden Time come from?

Golden Time was developed as part of an ecosystemic model of positive behaviour and values and is intrinsically linked to the Jenny Mosley Quality Circle Time model, although it may be used separately as an incentives system in its own right. In order to understand its roots, it is important to know a little of the context within which it grew and developed. For more detail on how to use the model, see Mosley, 1996 and 1998 (*Quality Circle Time* and *More Quality Circle Time*). See also the Inset training and accredited training in Appendix 4 (page 171–175).

Only if a whole-school community has proper training in the fundamentals will Quality Circle Time reach its full potential, and support the pupils and teachers in reaching theirs. The model is based on the principle of creating effective listening systems for adults and children within schools. It has been demonstrated to promote better relationships and more positive behaviour, which are two of the most effective improvements both to learning and the smooth and harmonious running of a school.

The Whole School Quality Circle Time model

This model interweaves a behaviour management system with a process of personal and social growth. Its premise is that the most effective way to promote positive behaviour and respectful relationships is through working on moral development within a structured Quality Circle Time approach.

The diagram on page 87 presents Quality Circle Time as a circular ecosystemic model.

The Whole School Quality Circle Time model

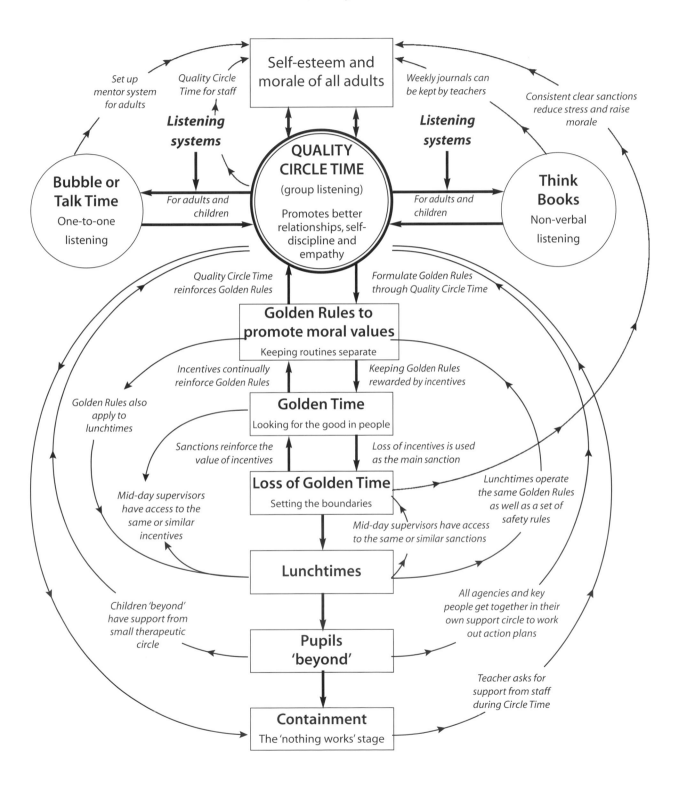

Some school leaders and class teachers reported that Circle Time experiences have enhanced their awareness of children's feelings and their own pedagogical needs. By listening to children they got to know them more quickly and raised their expectations as they witnessed personal, social and communications skill developments.

Through use of positive Circle Time pupils can develop self-esteem, listening and group-related social skills, and teachers and pupils can experience personal and social learning together.

Taylor, M. (2003) Going Round in Circles. *NFER*

A brief outline of the Whole School Quality Circle Time model

The Quality Circle Time model involves a commitment from schools to set up an ongoing process of circle meetings for adults and children, at which the key interpersonal and organisational issues that affect school development can be addressed. There are several key elements in the model:

- Improving the morale and self-esteem of staff.
- Three listening systems.
- The Golden Rules.
- Incentives.
- Sanctions through Golden Time.
- Lunchtime policy.
- Children 'beyond'.

It is not the intention to discuss all of these elements in detail in this chapter. Many of them are discussed elsewhere in this book and in other books on the subject (Mosley, 1989, 1993, 1996, 1998). However, some of the points here are worthy of further clarification, with the aim of making clear how Golden Time fits into the model.

Why do staff need their own listening systems?

Many teachers have come to feel in recent years that they are being asked simply to push children through academic hoops. They have lost that sense of relationship with children that originally drew them into teaching. Circle Time has the potential to help teachers reconnect with their original respect for children. If staff are to respond in a positive and warm manner to children, they need the ability to support each other as members of a team. The first focus of the Quality Circle Time training is on the emotional health of adults. That includes not only teachers and school managers, but also ancillary and support staff, as well as parents and carers. Adults commit themselves to working on their personal and professional development by engaging in regular Circle Times. Listening is put at the centre of the school timetable. The aim is to work on maintaining emotional safety, and to promote specific relationship skills.

What listening systems are available for the children?

Golden Time helps to foster a sense of community, and a key skill within a community is the ability of people to communicate with each other. Children need to practise these skills. The model provides for this.

Quality Circle Time sets up the following three systems within which children can speak with themselves and each other.

- **Circle Time.** This provides children with a weekly opportunity to experience positive relationships with other people. The games and exercises used are designed to foster a sense of community in the class, and to establish a safe boundary within which other activities can take place.

○ **Bubble Time and Talk Time.** These one-to-one listening systems, used in primary schools and secondary schools respectively, provide a private discussion between the teacher and pupils.

○ **Think Books.** These are offered as a daily non-verbal communication system. Every child is offered their own Think Book, which they do not have to use. They can scribble ideas or draw a picture in it, and put it in a special place for the teacher or teaching assistant to respond to. The books can take the heat out of a situation by allowing the child to express an emotion immediately, without having to resort to bad behaviour.

My class is a very 'spirited' group and Circle Time is a really good opportunity for us all to enjoy some peace and for the quieter children to have the opportunity to speak out in class. It also gives the socially 'less able' children something to think about – the way they treat others, the way things can upset others and so on.

It's been a great tool this year for bringing out into the open people's feelings, with many surprises – for me and for the class, I think. Children love Circle Time.

Jane Burrows, Class Teacher, Blackwell Primary School, Derbyshire

How the model helps create positive lunchtimes

An environment in which Golden Time will flourish helps to provide boundaries and positive incentives for children, even when they are not in the classroom. Lunchtimes can be distressing for children and adults alike if poor behaviour in the playground begins to become the norm.

Many children's behavioural problems stem from the fact that they do not know how to play with each other. Break times can be experiences of fear, loneliness and boredom. Feelings of being left out or picked on can be engendered and exacerbated. Those who supervise these breaks may feel beleaguered in the face of noisy, aggressive or frustrated children. Good practice involves creating opportunities for all children to join in a range of different activities. It also means providing quiet places for them to go. The model does not prescribe how children play, but it does encourage children to find activities that they enjoy and to find ways of relating to each other in caring and inclusive ways. See Mosley and Thorp (2002) for a comprehensive guide to creating happy playtimes.

Lunchtime strategies

The Quality Circle Time model requires that schools teach playground games. It encourages the zoning of the playground into activity areas that can be supervised by older children who have been appointed as members of Playground Patrols. A community taskforce can be formed of children who need to be constructively occupied. It suggests football parliaments are held in order to ensure that football contributes to the positive ethos of a school, rather than acting against it.

Links with Golden Time

In the model, mid-day supervisors are encouraged to use the Golden Time system, whilst also being invited to regular Circle Time meetings with children and members of staff. They have the right to use warning cards, which helps to reinforce the fact that there are rules to be obeyed, and that the rules are there for a reason.

All ancillary staff, once there is a whole-school positive lunchtime policy firmly in place, will have access to a warning and loss of Golden Time sanction system. Our experience was that initially children were inclined to misbehave with mid-day supervisory assistants, who would give their names into the class teacher so they would lose five minutes of Golden Time. The mid-day supervisors often found later that the child had earnt back the lost Golden Time. Our recommendation now is that the mid-day supervisor gives a visual warning by flashing a warning card; if the child breaks another rule their name is placed on a red Post-it note on the back of the warning card. They have a week to earn the Post-it back from the supervisor, in any way agreed on by both parties. If the child cannot be bothered to earn it back, then the supervisor hands the teacher the Post-it with the child's name on, and their teacher records it on the lost Golden Time sheet with an L (for lunchtime) next to it. The child is unable to earn it back from the teacher. A child cannot manipulate the system to their advantage.

When schools fail to develop a lunchtime policy, children will learn that moral values are only practised inside buildings with power. Outside in the playground, they see their own needs and the needs of other children being ignored. They are left to survive, in any way they can, in an emotionally barren wilderness.

Coming full circle

Once a school has practised all the key features of our model, it comes full circle. In other words, keeping the model vibrant and powerful means that adults need to sit in circles with each other and review their personal and professional progress. It is essential that if any problems are encountered at any time during the usage of the model, adults bring them to their staff Circle Time.

All adults need to be part of timetabled circle staff meetings. Our Golden Schools make sure that mid-day supervisors have two half-hour circle meetings each half-term. Teachers have one Circle Time staff meeting a half-term. Parents and administrative staff have one each term.

The greater the worth the school community places on Golden Time, the more the children will value it too.

To think about …

◆ Golden Time was developed within an ecosystemic model of positive behaviour and values and is intrinsically linked to Jenny Mosley's Quality Circle Time model, but it can be used as an effective incentives system in its own right.

◆ There are several key elements in the model:

> improving the morale and self-esteem of staff;
> Golden Rules;
> three listening systems;
> incentives;
> Golden Time;
> lunchtime policy;
> children 'beyond'.

◆ For more detailed information on how to use the model, refer to books that clearly explain it – for instance, Mosley (1996 and 1998).

◆ The Quality Circle Time model involves schools setting up an ongoing process of circle meetings for adults and children, at which the key interpersonal and organisational issues that affect school development can be addressed.

◆ Schools provide consistency within their behaviour-management systems by addressing behaviour outside the classroom; for example, in the playground.

8

The classroom where Golden Time thrives

Creating a golden classroom

Golden Time does not exist in a vacuum; it is part of a complex matrix of characters and cultures. It thrives within a culture of encouragement, where positive values are promoted and each child is celebrated. Classroom management in general is a key issue.

We, as teachers, need our own classroom-management techniques. In addition, we must consider the (sometimes uncomfortable) possibility that we may be causing some of the behaviour-management problems ourselves. If a teacher has tendencies towards the chaotic, lacking planning and organisation in activities and systems, children will become bored and frustrated. Our classroom rules need to be discussed, agreed upon and consistent. Our lessons need to be planned, made appropriate and adequately differentiated so that each child can experience challenge, success and achievement. Our teaching techniques need to be enlivening, diverse and informed. Our classrooms need to be bright, cheerful, imaginative and informative.

There are so many demands that it is hard to know where to start. We shall begin by saying that we may all be forgiven for not being perfect, and that we must be glad and celebrate all our successes as these indicate that we are doing a really good job.

There are many reasons why things may not be quite right yet. Perhaps a teacher is new to the profession and there are many tricks and ways still to be learnt. Maybe there is not enough time to get properly organised or ever really to catch up. The weight of new initiatives and the constantly changing academic environment may throw us once more, just as we thought we had reached a plateau on which we could succeed. Sometimes teachers are in need of a different type of Continuing Professional Development than that commonly on offer. Until our classroom and behaviour-management techniques have reached our own chosen level of proficiency, we might not feel the need for advanced batik, further touch rugby or improvement in our interactive whiteboard technique. Sometimes we just need help with the classroom and the children, and we need the help now.

We need to look after ourselves and our needs, both physical and emotional, too. Self-care is sometimes overlooked when we are planning our teaching activities, but it is as important as many of the other factors. It affects our energy, creativity, resilience and tolerance. How often during a typical day do we call upon, and even rely upon, all of these strengths? If you have 'gone off' children or lost the enjoyment of their company and had to jump through too many academic hoops, then maybe you need to bring some fun elements back into the classroom.

Fortunately, there are many useful tips for reducing the types and frequencies of disruptive incidences that occur in the classroom. These tips are intrinsically linked to Golden Time, which thrives in the environment of a caring and comprehensive classroom system.

The following checklists are only pointers in the right direction – truly, each mini-section could generate a book in its own right. If you are encouraged to think along the line suggested and they appeal to you, you will be able to ferret out courses and books to satisfy your need to know more.

It is a well-known but little-celebrated fact that teachers are complete gold-mines of skills and knowledge about everything – including how to motivate, decorate, contemplate, negotiate, appreciate, celebrate, ameliorate, mediate, dedicate and delegate. However, for those returning to teach or starting to teach, and those who would simply welcome a reminder in black and white, here are some checklists from teachers themselves.

Let's start at the beginning.

The new school year

The first few weeks that a new class is with you are when you determine the future climate of the classroom and establish the ground rules. Children need to be given the security of boundaries to enable them to flourish. This is the ideal time for the Golden Rules and Golden Time partnership to be introduced, if it has not been a part of your children's previous school life.

Key questions for helping to get your new year off to a good start

- Have I introduced the Golden Rules through Circle Time and made sure that the children have had time to discuss them fully?

- Have I asked the children for ideas of routines to help the class run smoothly?

- Are the children familiar with all the daily routines – where and how to line up, toilet procedures, break and lunchtime routines, playground routines, beginning and ending the day?

- Have we agreed on the signs and signals that I could use in the classroom?

- Have we agreed upon our vision of a happy classroom of caring children in which everyone feels safe and valued?

- Have I explained to the children about Golden Time and let them all experience fully the first, wonderful Golden Time session?

- Most important, am I able to be friendly and welcoming every day?

How golden is my classroom?

The working environment in which you and the children spend the day is important to everyone. Keeping it a golden, upbeat and stimulating one which is clean and fresh and welcoming, with changing displays, will provide a head start for all who work there.

Key questions for a positive classroom

- Is my classroom bright and attractive?

  This will help considerably to lighten the atmosphere.

- Are my displays effective and up to date?
  Get rid of any shabby displays, put up bright new backing paper and mount children's work soon after it is done.

- Do I change the displays regularly throughout the year?
  Use drapes and double mounting in complementary colours.

- Have I displayed photographs of children working well together and on their own?
  Children need visual reminders to show them how diligent they have been.

○ Have I made an attractive display somewhere with all the children's names on it?

A picture with each name on a leaf on a tree, or a positive statement with each name written next to it, helps to increase cohesiveness and create a positive identity.

○ Have I displayed attainment targets for each child – for example, on rockets set for the moon, or footballs in front of a goal?

Targets in an attractive, appropriate setting will receive attention from the children.

○ Could I display more art and design work?

It will make a stunning addition to the look of the room.

○ Could I use posters, old wildlife calendars or real flowers and plants to brighten empty spaces?

Children get real pleasure from nature and nature walks, and it is good to bring a little nature into your classroom.

○ Could I use a three-dimensional display to add depth to the room?

A small shelf or table at the base of a display board can open up all sorts of opportunities.

○ Do I regularly refresh the atmosphere by opening a window, even on a cold day, to replenish the oxygen?

Children and adults will become tired if the air becomes stale.

○ Do I sometimes use music to set the tone?

Examples are calm music for coming in after play, uplifting music to help with a particular transition time or changing for PE.

Move them round

Where the children sit may have a profound effect on their attention, listening and watching, and on their following the Golden Rules – all of which affect their learning. They may be more or less disruptive when sitting with certain others, and this can greatly influence their concentration. Thank goodness for all those children who are able to switch off the distractions of the room and get down to their activities.

Key questions for seating arrangements and moving children around

○ Do I regularly change the seating arrangements to try different combinations of children working together?
This helps prevent children becoming stuck in socially linked behaviour patterns.

○ Can all the children see me and the board easily?
If seats are facing away from you, ask the children to stand up and turn their seats around when you are addressing the whole class.

○ Could I pair up a child who has difficulty in staying focused with a reliable child who can?
A peer often has a far greater effect than an adult.

○ Could I change the seating arrangements for some lessons to encourage children to form more relationships within the group?
Children sometimes need a reason to interact with others.

○ Have I tried placing a child who can be disruptive in a well-behaved, hard-working group?
This may have an amazing effect on that child's behaviour. The desire to be accepted gradually overrides the child's original needs as they come to identify with their new group. Beware; you know that the converse may be true too.

Silence is golden

A little calm in the classroom can go a very long way. It helps children to have time to reflect, and provides a few golden moments for you all. Consider some of the following ways in which you could contribute to the creation of calm in your classroom.

Key questions for a calm classroom

○ Do I begin my day in a positive way, with an established calming routine for when the children enter?
Remember, you help set the scene.

○ Do the children know that when they come in, they are going to hang up their 'playground' selves with their coats and become classroom children?
Use visual tactics like this to reinforce your positive behaviour points.

⊙ Have I organised an ordered procedure for entering the classroom?
If the children are to sit on the carpet, a question or sum could be written on the board each day for them to think about in silence – for example, 'What would your dream holiday be?'

⊙ Do the children have a piece of work they can continue if I have a short job to do?
Cartoon strips, pictures, word searches and problem solving are good.

⊙ Do I use music to set the scene and provide a calming and thoughtful addition to the atmosphere?
If you can, keep a range of music handy, clearly labelled for different occasions.

⊙ Have I thought about having children who find it difficult to stay focused near me when seated on the carpet?
You can then remind them with a gentle touch and a whisper, without a fuss.

⊙ Could I encourage children to be still by asking them to pretend they are something?
Choose still items, like statues, rocks, or sleeping lions, or play listening games.

⊙ Do I ask children questions by name to help them to keep attentive?
When a child hears their own name, it should help to re-engage them.

⊙ Do I incorporate some physical activity into carpet time to help those who find it hard to sit still?
Even a brief 'stand up and shake' or some arm movements, like writing something in the air, will help.

Lining up calmly

Go for the positive, not the negative. Lining-up times can be some of the most stressful times of the day, and they contribute to setting the scene for the next lesson. These are the times when excitement and bustle may encourage children to break the Golden Rules and lose Golden Time. If this applies to your class, try some of the suggestions below.

Key questions for a quiet line

⊙ Do I use the strategy of asking the children to think of something while lining up?

This could be a poem or rhyme that they all know well. Ask them to say the rhyme in their heads without making a sound. Ask random children what the next word they can think of is.

○ Could I ask the children to think of a favourite place and visualise the journey to it?

○ Do I ask the children to think of something specific when they line up?
For example, they could imagine that they are going on a picnic. They need to make a mental list of the food and drink they would like to take. Ask one or two children to tell you one item they have thought of.

○ Could I tell the children to imagine they are soldier ants?
They have to line up perfectly quietly, hands by their sides, faces to the front, then walk as a regiment.

If things go wrong

There will always be times when disaster strikes – those times, for instance, when the video player breaks down, the room you intended to use is occupied or you are suddenly asked to teach a different class. These are times when children may become frustrated and excitable, and they may push the rules to the limit. To prevent some of these moments of frustration occurring, consider some of the following ideas.

Key questions for those difficult times

○ Have I got a few lessons prepared as contingencies, ready to fall back on?
Photocopied sets and problem-solving activities can be immediately available.

○ Do I make sure my children have informal, on-going pieces of work to hand?
Puzzles or pictures are something that the children can easily pick up and can be a useful standby for chaotic moments. Crosswords are great for older children; some may like a blank grid and the challenge of designing one themselves.

○ Have I considered using maths coordinate pictures on squared paper?
These can be very useful for older primary-age children. Whereas some children draw a picture using the coordinates they have been given, others can draw a picture and write the coordinates for others to draw.

○ Do I remember to remain calm and relaxed?
It is usually pointless to display disappointment or anger in front of the children.

> Do I apologise to the children for their disappointment and assure them that I will hold the intended lesson at the earliest convenient time?
>
> *By considering the children's feelings, you are modelling considerate behaviour.*

Effective lesson management

Effective teaching requires juggling many different skills. Within a Golden Class, you all need to be very clear about what each lesson is about. The children will trust that you will challenge them and guarantee a level of success so that they can taste and feel achievement. It is imperative to use plenty of praise and encouragement, and to recognise any effort. For example, if you ask a child to do something and they comply with your request, try to avoid being drawn into criticising secondary behaviour such as loud sighs whilst complying. Ignore these – you have accomplished your goal and can always have a quiet word with them after the lesson.

In addition to all this, accept that different people learn in different ways. Lessons should be presented using a variety of learning media and techniques, to give each child a fair chance.

Key questions for lesson management

> Am I clear about the learning objectives – have I shared these with the children?

> Do the children understand why they are studying particular lessons and how they fit into the general scheme of learning?

> Have I used the most appropriate grouping for each lesson?

> Have I allotted the correct amount of time to each task?

> Do I differentiate work for the different ability groups in a way that makes sense?

> Have I organised my materials and equipment efficiently so that I do not waste time hunting for things?

> Do I look at the children when talking to them and address individuals from time to time, asking for feedback, and commending them for good listening or sitting?

> Does my voice convey interest in and enthusiasm for the lesson that I am teaching?

- Do I use rewards effectively?
- Have I ensured that the noise level and movement around the classroom are acceptable for the task in hand and not causing disruption?
- Do I move around the classroom making positive comments throughout the lesson?
- Have I explored different learning styles?

A reminder of the key learning styles

> ***Try to plan for all three learning styles in your teaching.***

- **Visual.** Children who learn visually will relate best to written information, diagrams, notes and pictures.
- **Auditory.** Children who learn best in the auditory style benefit from the spoken word. It can be helpful for them to read their work aloud in order to understand its meaning.
- **Kinaesthetic.** This style of learning involves physical movement. The child learns best by touching, through movement or by actually doing what they are learning about.

Hang on to your 'golden' expectations

Although many teachers set out with great expectations of their children, it is easy to lose many of them by the wayside. Try to keep high expectations for your children – it does play a crucial role in encouraging positive behaviour and boosting self-esteem. It may be difficult, especially if you have heard discouraging reports about a child and they come to you with an established reputation. You may find it helpful to ask yourself the following questions. Above all, have faith.

Key questions for keeping golden expectations

- ◯ Do I keep a check on my attitude to the children – do I respect and like them?

- ◯ Do I allow sufficient time for my expectations to replace the previously low ones that have influenced a child?

- ◯ Am I discouraged if I seem to be making little progress?

- ◯ Do I realise that if I keep believing, my approach will work in time?

- ◯ Do I treat inappropriate behaviour as transitory, not part of a child's character?

- ◯ Do I talk about the behaviour, not the child – for example, 'I want to talk to you about your behaviour at lunchtime'?

- ◯ Do I tell the child frequently that I have faith in them to do the right thing?

- ◯ Do I praise the child frequently when they make a positive response – for example, 'Well done, Liam, for putting your hand up and not calling out'?

- ◯ Do I reaffirm the positive behaviour when it wavers – 'Liam, I will be able to choose you when you put your hand up quietly'?

- ◯ Do I tell the child of the good progress they have made, recalling the former behaviour that they have left behind?
  Children love to hear confirmation that their 'negative' selves are a feature of the past.

- ◯ Do I often expect a particular child to disregard my instructions?
  If so, your attitude and body language convey the message and you get the result that you expect.

- ◯ Along with keeping my expectations high, am I keeping a measure of realism in terms of work or behaviour from certain children?

Parents as partners

How often do we hear a teacher complaining that parents don't seem particularly bothered about their child's inappropriate behaviour, or that they don't turn up for parents' evenings or are hostile when they do? It may be helpful to imagine yourself in their shoes and consider how you would feel if you heard only negative reports about your child. Wouldn't you move into fight or flight too? Changing a parent's perception of their child in school can have a hugely positive impact on the child. Informing your parents about Golden Time and the reasoning behind your incentives and sanctions system can help them to understand the way in which you are choosing to work. Remember, some parents may have had an unhappy school experience. Below are some further suggestions.

Key questions for working with parents as partners

- First, do I regularly find good news to tell a parent?
  If you can, focus on the positive for a while – feed back on any small target that has been reached.

- Do I try to commend the child to the parent for a good piece of work, an occasion when the child sat or listened well or a kind action the child performed?
  Parents may be well aware of the negative aspects of their child's behaviour, so unless it is necessary that you inform them of an incident, avoid spreading bad news.

- Can I remember to give the parent something to be happy about repeatedly so that they can be pleased with their child?
  This can, over time, result in both parent and child coming into school with a far more positive attitude.

- Do I share my positive behaviour-management policy with the parents via a meeting, newsletter or web page?
  Once they understand what you are trying to achieve and how you are trying to achieve it, they may be more willing to support the system.

- Could I suggest to the parent that they might be the best reward for the child?
  We have learnt over the years that, more than anything, children yearn for a bit of time when their parent plays with them. Allowing the child to take home the class's favourite game to share with the parent is a thrilling reward.

Building self-esteem

Fundamental to your children displaying positive behaviour is the building of their self-esteem. This is especially important for those children with lower abilities or physical impairments, and those who come from different cultures.

You need to be aware of the very beneficial influence that you can have in raising self-esteem by showing a child that you like and value them. Using the Golden Rules and Golden Time as an incentive helps boost children's self-esteem, because they receive recognition for even the smallest efforts that they make, and receive regular good news about themselves as people.

Key questions for supporting children in building their self-esteem

- Does the child know that I value them as an individual and that I am pleased that they are part of the class?
  This will help them feel they belong and are not 'outside' the class.

- Do I focus on building positive relationships and establishing good rapport with each child?
  If you show care towards a child, they will be more likely to want to please you and do the right thing.

- Am I aware that I play a crucial role in modelling to other children and adults how any particular child should be treated?
  If you react with frustration, impatience, irritation, sarcasm or other negative responses, these will be copied.

- Can I try, if I lose my patience and react negatively to a child's behaviour, to repair the relationship?
  Restoring harmony is in your best interests as well as the child's.

- Do I specifically create moments of success and praise them loudly?
  Moments like these will not necessarily happen by themselves, but they can be great mood-lifters and self-esteem boosters when you make them happen.

The importance of the language we use

The language we use, and the way that we use it, have profound effects within the classroom. How you talk to children affects their whole lives. Turning negative statements into positive ones brightens up the day, setting a scene in which Golden Time and positive classroom initiatives blossom. Negative language is infectious. If you also think about the power of suggestion, you will realise that it is far better to suggest something positive than something negative. For people interested in neurolinguistic programming (NLP) this will be especially interesting to explore.

Language can be a bridge of communication, or a barrier. It creates real problems for some children, especially when English is a foreign language to them.

And many other children suffer because of poor language skills. Children with an impoverished vocabulary are often unable to engage in complex thinking, and it is difficult for them to form relationships with more articulate children. They lack this valuable source of help to improve their language skills, and they often bond with similar children, with whom they feel more comfortable. They may not be able to tell you how they really feel, and if problems arise with work or behaviour, they may use language that does not accurately convey what they are experiencing. They might say they hate school or school is boring, when the reality is that they feel isolated and fearful.

If you have children with poor language skills in your class, think about how you can make your teaching more accessible to them. Perhaps the use of a teaching assistant with a prepared and simplified script would be appropriate. Put your rules into their language – along with photographs to illustrate the rules.

- The Golden Rules can be referred to when you wish to reinforce positive behaviour:

  'Well done, Saba, for listening well!'

- The Golden Rules can be used as a reminder for the behaviour that you want to see:

  'Remember, children, we do work hard and we don't waste time.'

- The Golden Rules can be used to point out inappropriate behaviour:

  'When you know you hurt someone, can you tell me which Golden Rule you are breaking? Yes, that's right, we are gentle, we don't hurt others.'

Key questions for using positive language

- Do I think about the language that I use?
  'Are you going to give Saba back her book?' only provides an opportunity for a negative answer.

- Do I use open invitations for poor behaviour?
  If you say, 'Do that again and I'll send you out', would-be escapees may repeat their offence.

- Do I try not to 'blow my top' and shout?

- Am I positive and generous with praise?
  We should blast children with praise.

- Do I remember to thank children for doing something well?

- Am I aware that more than one person giving instructions or making demands can be confusing and upsetting to a child?

- Do I remember that making immediate demands for emotionally difficult actions – such as saying sorry – are unwise?

- Do I remind the children of positive behaviour before they do something inappropriate?

- Do I give praise regularly and make positive comments throughout a lesson?

- Do I try not to mix praise with criticism?
  An example is 'That is a neat piece of work but you'll have to work on your spellings' – the child will remember only the criticism.

- Do I give positive and active attention when I am listening?

- Do I say sorry if I have been unfair or given an unclear explanation?

- Do I remember not to interrupt children when they are speaking, and try to pick up on unspoken clues as to what they are really trying to tell me?

- Do I remember never to put labels on a child – for example, bully, naughty – as labels stick?
  Instead, label the behaviour: 'Your behaviour was poor in the dining hall.'

- Do I try to avoid being drawn into arguments?
  It is better to repeat a request calmly until a child responds, telling them that you will discuss the matter further later.

- Do I speak to a child in private about their behaviour?
  It may be best to wait until after the lesson, or go to one side of the room.

The value of using prepared scripts

Prepared scripts are valuable tools that can prevent situations from escalating. They elicit the response that you require, whereas an ill-conceived comment might result in a negative outcome. If you respond to a child when you are angry, you may say something in the heat of the moment that you later regret or that has long-lasting implications. Some useful examples of using scripts are shown below. Take care that your tone of voice does not convey a different message from the one you are saying, and be aware that the tone you use may give the same statement different meanings to a child. For example, 'Come on' may be said encouragingly, impatiently, angrily and so on. Try to keep your voice neutral and calm. Using an appropriate tone of voice is essential for the positive use of prepared scripts.

Some examples of how positive language may be used

- ● 'What are you doing, Megan? What should you be doing?'
- ● 'Maybe you are looking for a pencil, Bradley, and [not 'but'] now will you sit down and continue with your work?'
- ● 'Is that a sensible place to sit, Charlie?' (Children are remarkably honest about this.)
- ● 'Where would be a good place to sit?'
- ● 'How could you use the paints carefully, Morgan?'
- ● 'Parriel, playtime is the right time to discuss a television programme. You need to get on with your numeracy task now.'
- ● 'Joe, if you talk that loudly I can't help Matthew. Please keep the noise down.'
- ● 'Sophie, I can see that you are not working. Do you need help?'
- ● 'Fabian, you seem to be having a difficult time today. What could help you to work?'
- ● 'Jordan, remember our rule for respectful language.'
- ● 'Ellie, if you continue to chatter to your neighbours, you will have to sit on your own.'
- ● 'Ryan, if you choose to play with that toy during lesson time, I will have to look after it until you go home today.'

> *If you follow a request with a 'thank you' and then turn away, you have implied to the child that you know they will comply. This is a positive action which allows them some 'take-up' time.*

A calm ending

It is really nice to be able to send the children out in a positive frame of mind to meet their parents. If time allows, try to share a short ending ritual with them before you part company.

Suggestions for a calm ending

- At the end of the day, ask the children to close their eyes and think of one thing that they have really enjoyed in school that day.

- Occasionally make the time to say goodbye to each child and wish them a nice evening.

- Before they leave the classroom, ask the children to stand up and breathe in and out slowly five times. While they do this, ask them to imagine a nice, warm, happy feeling.

- In a music lesson, the children could compose their own short, uplifting class song that could be sung at the end of each day. This would help each child positively identify with the group before going home.

- Try to time it well. Not leaving enough time to pack up means that you and the children are always flustered at the end of the day. Leaving too much time might mean that the children are waiting too long with their coats and bags on and left in limbo, tempting poor behaviour.

Looking after yourself

We cannot overemphasise how, as a person who works in a school, it is vitally important to look after yourself first. We all have limited amounts of energy and personal reserves. If we continually use these up without stopping to replenish them, then we are 'running on empty'. This is not a sustainable state in the longer term, or a desirable state to be in for the shorter term. It may lead to a lack of resilience or even ill-health. Study the following questions. If you answer the majority of them negatively, you may be pushing yourself too hard. You may not believe in your own sense of worth.

Key questions for self-care

- Do I give myself the same care and attention that I give to others?
- Do I realise that I am not an endless resource for others and remember that I must stock up on reserves and not get drained?
- Do I remember that I have needs too, which may be different from my family's, my friends', or my colleagues'?
- Can I remember that I do not have to say 'yes' to all requests or feel guilty if I say 'no'?
- Do I remember that the perfect person does not exist, and that making mistakes is permissible? I can learn from them, as can others.
- Do I know that I can't solve all the problems I am confronted with – that I can only do my best?
- Do I always remember that I have the right to be treated with respect as a worthwhile, intelligent and competent person?
- Am I aware that I do not have to have everyone's approval all of the time to know that I am trying my hardest?
- Can I prioritise some time for unwinding, as time for unwinding is time well spent?

(Adapted from Mosley, 1993)

To think about …

◆ Golden Time thrives in a Golden Classroom, where positive strategies, encouragement and celebration are a must.

◆ There may be areas in your classroom where you could modify your practice to make a real difference to your class. Important areas to consider include:

- getting the new school year off to a great start;
- creating a pleasant and practical atmosphere in your classroom;
- seating the children effectively;
- knowing how you re-create calm;
- understanding how to encourage children to line up calmly;
- knowing what to do if the unexpected happens;
- managing lessons effectively;
- keeping high expectations for all children;
- making partners of your children's parents;
- helping the children build sound self-esteem;
- thinking about the language you use;
- using positive language as much as possible;
- knowing and using prepared scripts;
- creating a calm end to the day;
- most importantly, looking after yourself.

Constructive Circle Times are a valuable part of Golden Time.

A school display supporting Golden Time.

Choosing Golden Time Club activities.

Operating Golden Time using the sun and cloud approach.

Golden Rules shared in assembly.

The dressing-up box is a popular Golden Time choice.

Board games on the playground are a favourite Golden Time activity.

The Juggling Club is great for developing co-ordination.

A Golden Time picnic can be a group celebration.

Golden Time parachute games can be played inside and outside.

Using a warning card can be a discreet visual cue.

Puppets are popular in Golden Time.

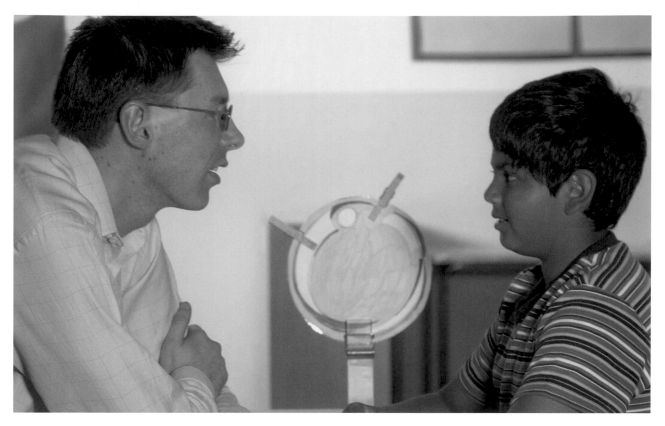

This school has adapted Bubble Time – an effective listening system.

A gardening club is an enjoyable Golden Time activity.

The Golden Peace Table has been used in this school.

Headteacher's golden awards.

A child sharing his Headteacher's Award with a friend.

Effective lunchtimes assist the use of Golden Time.

Table of the Week is a Golden Time lunchtime strategy.

Using a sand timer for a child who has lost Golden Time.

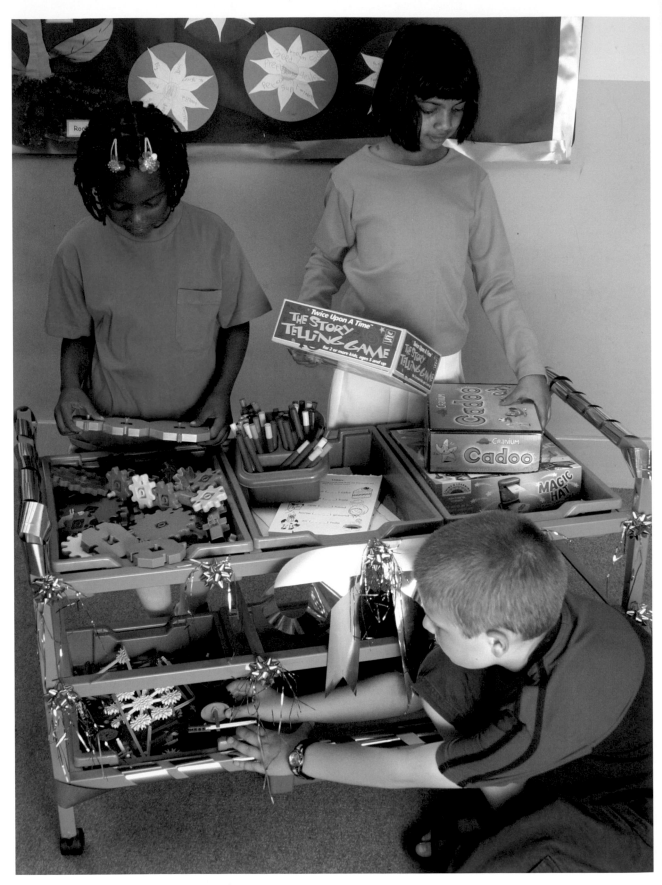

A golden trolley will keep your activities neat and tidy.

A school visitor participating in Golden Time.

Celebrating with Golden Time awards.

Special child of the week.

9

Questions people ask

Many of the following questions have been asked on the National College of School Leadership Internet site called Talking Heads. Headteachers have asked Jenny Mosley, in the hotseat, to answer these questions. All the questions come from headteachers and class teachers on the front line of Golden Time practice who are seeking answers to practical questions about the model. We hope you benefit from their experiences and the answers they received.

Is Golden Time still the best reward system?

Q I am head of a junior school in Devon. Two years ago one of your colleagues worked with us to develop improved systems of Circle Time and behaviour management. Best thing we ever did – especially the whole-staff day later on when we looked at ways to improve our own esteem and well-being so that we were at our best in working day-to-day with quite challenging children. We implemented Golden Time and have been consistent in our use of this strategy alongside the Golden Rules. We revisit regularly, reviewing progress. Is Golden Time still the best reward system? Have you developed any other rewards?

A We invest a lot of time in working with whole-school staffs on raising their energy levels and developing their own self-esteem first – otherwise it is almost impossible to help them respond positively to challenging pupils. In some schools we go to, teachers have become so tired that their own behaviour is really very challenging. In these instances we are likely to bring in yoga teachers and masseurs to help the staff first.

Golden Time certainly reduces teachers' stress levels as they do not have to use up all their energy on being cross or disappointed. They can just calmly put down a warning card . . . I think Golden Time is the core system – but it needs constant overhauling and shining up to make it truly, sparkly golden. We constantly have review circles with pupils to have a round of 'one thing that would make Golden Time better'. We need to bring in different people from the community to celebrate – sixth formers can come in and work with the pupils, learning mentors can come in and play football during Golden Time. It needs to be the most exciting weekly community effort.

Golden Time certificates are a key as well. These constantly reinforce with parents the importance of the Golden Rules as these are printed on the certificates. Some schools move on to creating Golden Time clubs. The only thing you have to watch there is that you don't put the children who lose Golden Time into a separate room – this will become the Sin Club which some children with low self-esteem will subscribe to as it gives them a temporary notoriety. Make sure that the empty table with the sand timer is alongside the actual club that the child would have been in if they hadn't chosen to lose that privilege.

Don't forget that we try to help children back from the brink of losing Golden Time by talking through how they can use their earning back contract – our job is to see if there are any children beyond this approach (there will be very few). There are some children who need some extra therapeutic support. Regarding your question about whether there are any other incentives, we do use a range of parallel incentive systems. These are best described in *Turn Your School Round*, pages 28–32 [Mosley, 1993]. Amongst these is the Happy Family Tree – it is one of my favourites. You can either use a real branch in a pot or cut out a tree and put it on a wall. The children receive golden leaves for any Golden Rules they have kept, such as being gentle or honest. Golden leaves lead to a golden acorn and three golden acorns lead to a red squirrel . . . isn't life abundant and amazing!

Shouldn't we be encouraging intrinsic rather than extrinsic rewards?

Q Like many other contributors, I am already a convert to Circle Time and have a firm belief that you raise standards by raising self-esteem. I do have some small doubts, though, creeping in about rewards . . . I want the self-esteem of the children, staff and parents to develop from within, so we have stopped giving stickers, smiley faces and so on. Instead we encourage children to put themselves forward by saying what they are good at and how proud they are of themselves. One member of staff has suggested that Golden Time is a reward and as such should be stopped. I agree that it is an entitlement. I'd like to hear any comments you may have on this.

A There is a huge debate about extrinsic and intrinsic rewards. I do not subscribe to the theory that extrinsic rewards prevent children from moving towards an inner locus of control; I believe they create the right ethos in which children can move towards esteeming their own work and relationships. In an early book I wrote about how children should be encouraged during Circle Time to bring to the circle any piece of work for which they wished to award themselves a special dot – or they could draw a picture of behaviour that they had engaged in which they were proud of. As long as they could justify their choice, they were entitled to receive their own special reward. But more importantly than this – in step 4 of the five-step Circle Time model, we have a script for teachers to use to encourage children to nominate other children who are very calm, create a lovely working atmosphere by not shouting out, are learning to walk away from fights and so on. Once they are nominated, if the majority of the class agree (which 95 per cent of the time they do), something called a Class Team Honours Certificate is awarded [see page 52]. If the child or the class don't feel they quite deserve the certificate yet, the child places themselves on the achievement ladder at what they feel is the appropriate rung. Golden Time is a different issue. It shouldn't be earned – the children should walk in shining with it on a Monday morning because the whole school trusts them to keep the Golden Rules. In this way every 'middle-plodder child' receives their just entitlement. It is an entitlement because, as I explain to the children, if they keep to the Golden Rules, they save the teacher and the mid-day supervisor so much time that it is only fair that they are allowed to enjoy that time by celebrating together once a week.

Is Golden Time humiliating?

Q A conversation I had today has set me thinking – it goes like this.

'We don't believe in humiliating the children in front of others, do we?'
'No.'
'So isn't sitting waiting for your time up before Golden Time just the same as standing the "naughty" children up in assembly?'

I must admit I found this one difficult to answer. What do I say?

A An essential feature of the model is that we give a visual warning before a child loses five minutes of Golden Time. The younger children have a golden sun, followed by a golden sun with a cloud going over its face, followed by a sad cloud. When a child breaks a Golden Rule, their peg from the golden sun is put on the warning cloud and we ask the question – 'Do you want to come back to the Golden Rules by stopping that kicking: or do you want to break another Golden Rule, go to the sad cloud and lose one minute of Golden Time?' With older children the yellow warning card is on the wall with a statement above that says 'Behaviour is your choice.' Then an arrow goes from one side of the warning to a bubble that says 'Break another rule and you lose five minutes' Golden Time' and another arrow leads to a bubble that says 'Come back to the Golden Rules and we will celebrate in Golden Time.' Children must learn that behaviour is their choice. The whole model concentrates on helping children move towards their inner locus of control – where they learn to take responsibility for their actions and the consequences of those actions. When they have lost five minutes, or one minute, and are looking at a sand timer, they will be very clear – if the visual warnings are properly carried out – that they chose that consequence. They are reflecting on their behaviour – they are reflecting on the fact that they have lost a part of their privilege – and that this was their choice. So, I believe that sanctions uphold the self-esteem of children because they give them safe boundaries and show them that adults care enough about them to put the consequences into action. If there were no visual warning I would not be so confident. If there is only a verbal warning, given that one in five children has a high level of chaos in their mind, it is highly likely they will not hear the verbal warning . . . and then, yes, life would seem unfair. But with the above system it is explicit, clear, visual and therefore they chose the consequence. Also they never lose all their Golden Time. If they have blown it all on Monday, they get the opportunity to use the earning back contract [see page 151]. So they have that choice also.

If a child is unable to work within this system, it may well be that their level of inner chaos is so high that they have moved into the child 'beyond' category and need to work on Tiny Achievable Tickable Targets [see page 156].

How does Golden Time relate to playground behaviour and mid-day supervisor support?

Q We have a great school. The staff and children are superb! However, our playground is tiny and pretty bleak. We have worked really hard to ensure that playtimes are stimulating for the children. We have worked with Year 6 children to paint school murals, provided play equipment such as juggling balls, as suggested by the School Council – seeing 300 balls being juggled at a playtime is interesting – skipping ropes, quoits, hoops, large balls, softballs, and beanies. The School Council meet regularly each half-term. We worked with a consultant from Jenny Mosley's team and picked up good ideas, and we have Circle Time as a regular feature of the timetable. Obviously when issues arise we use Circle Time to discuss these. But time after time, despite training the mid-day supervisors in positive behaviour, mutual respect, not shouting or accusing pupils (they have had training at least three times with LEA consultants from the Healthy Schools team, the deputy and outside consultants), and having regular half-termly meetings with the deputy or myself, we still find that their way of working with the children does not improve and so the issues of playground behaviour are still appearing at lunchtime. What else can we do? How can we get our dear ladies to listen and take note of how we want them to behave, because at the moment they are helping to create the negative culture that exists at lunchtime? Help!

A You describe a wonderful approach and attitude to firming up a really exciting lunchtime policy. You deserve to have peaceful, productive and respectful lunchtimes, but it's still not happening for you all. Why is it that sometimes, despite our best efforts with the admin support or teaching staff, there appears to be no personal growth or sharing of the school vision? One of my theories hinges on self-esteem. If an adult has low self-esteem, personal change is extraordinarily difficult. People with low self-esteem often ride roughshod over other people's feelings. If you felt good about yourself, you would not need to talk disrespectfully to other people. However, because you are giving so much input to them, your irritation and disappointment at their lack of response may be more apparent than you realise. It goes against the grain, but somehow, despite feeling let down, you have to keep looking for the tiny markers of success they may have achieved. Feeding these back to them in verbal praise or written notes, ending your lunchtime meetings with 'One positive thing I have noticed about lunchtimes', might go a little way towards softening their attitudes. Sometimes, when I work on my own with mid-day supervisors, they have a list of moans to do with the fact that they don't feel they are communicated with properly. Some, who are not parents, don't get the letters about what's going on in the school. Sometimes the teachers let them down by not picking the kids up from the playground on time. Sometimes the dining-hall system goes wrong because teachers don't let the children out quickly enough (I was the worst culprit at this). There are quite often a series of small events which have added to their perception of not being valued.

It becomes a vicious circle; they become more truculent and strident – we withhold our warmth and valuing response; we become emotionally colder – they feel less a part of the whole ethos. Have you asked mid-day supervisors to class Circle Times? When they are not locked into the interaction, and can observe or take part in a Circle Time on 'How we can make lunchtimes better', they are often amazed at the gentleness and wisdom of children. They don't usually have a chance to see them behaving like that. When we do these Circle Time sessions, we often ask the children, in front of the mid-day supervisors, 'What does a mid-day supervisor do that makes you feel good and safe?' By keeping the dialogue very safe, mid-day supervisors are made to feel praised and valued. We also give them 'Gold Dust notes', on which they can write positive comments about the individual progress of difficult children and the good behaviour of the majority of children, then pop them into the class's Golden News Post-box. Another strategy they like is to be given Golden Raffle tickets. At every opportunity, whenever they see any good behaviour (you need to identify a list of good behaviours, such as lining up calmly, displaying good manners and so on), they hand the child a raffle ticket with the child's name and the words 'good choice' on it. The pupils then put their raffle tickets into a big drum, which is brought onto the stage at a Friday assembly as the weekly mid-day supervisors' celebration of great lunchtime behaviour. A child then does a loud drum roll, a hand plunges into the raffle tickets and draws one out, and a hush goes over the crowd. A prize is awarded, a huge cheer erupts . . . and the mid-day supervisors' self-esteem is lifted a little. There are lots of other ideas in *Turn Your School Round*, but you may have tried them all. The learning I still find the hardest to swallow is that, despite the fact that I have been as warm and positive as I can be (or, at least, I think I have), I still cannot win all people over. Sometimes you may have to go down a more radical route. Some schools will tell you they have raised money through the PTA and have bought in paid play leaders. Some schools have bought in trained sixth formers. It's an ongoing long-term task to solve this problem and, as I said at the beginning, you all deserve to succeed.

What are the most important factors for emotional safety?

Q What would you consider the five most important things a school can do to achieve emotionally safe classrooms?

A The first step towards an emotionally safe classroom is an emotionally safe teacher. In other words, teachers need to understand that they are the most powerful barometer of the emotional temperature of a class. It's a truism to say that your mood affects the mood of everyone around you. When I am running training days, I talk a lot about the fact that there are days when even you know that you are too dangerous to go out. On those days, I say to people, 'Don't try to do an exciting Circle Time or anything different – just get through the day with dignity and treats.' We as consultants often help teachers work out how to put Golden Moments into their day and how to create their own personal care programme.

The second step would be to work out, with your pupils, the moral values you all wish to adopt to keep your classroom physically and emotionally safe. We call these Golden Rules. When the Golden Rules are displayed, they are backed with gold paper for maximum effect. We take photos of children keeping the Golden Rules (the ideas from the photos being suggested by the pupils themselves). In other words, we would have photos of children being gentle, kind, honest, listening, working hard and looking after property. At step 3, you then need to work with the pupils separately on the routines of the class, which we call class rules: 'We put our pens and pencils away in the box', 'We line up calmly' and so on. These are the safety routines. They keep order . . . but they must not be muddled up with the moral values.

Once these rules are established, work out a clearly consistent, transparent and fair system of incentives and sanctions. Again, these need to be negotiated with the class, and they need to reflect the language of the Golden Rules. Examples are 'An emotionally safe classroom rewards children who look after other people's emotions', 'Safe classrooms have rewards for children who are gentle, kind and honest' and so on. Your sanctions, to be emotionally safe, need to be based on sound psychological principles. We advocate the withdrawal of Golden Time, a privilege that is available to all children to enable them to celebrate all those pupils who keep to the moral values. The Golden Time system has been structured particularly with the needs of 'middle-plodders' in mind. In other words, an emotionally safe classroom does not just focus on disruptive pupils. It concentrates its resources and its energy on all those children who come in every day and keep to the ethos of the class. I am taking it for granted that an emotionally safe class teacher would only offer children a curriculum that enabled each one of them to experience success and excitement.

The final step is to ensure that the weekly forum of Circle Time is vibrant and fun. I have seen some very boring Circle Times in which the children sit in a circle and the teacher talks too much. To do Circle Time properly, the teacher would adhere to a five-step structure which would not only allow every child to be heard, but it would also ensure that the class celebrated success. The overriding ethos would be that this circle was an exciting and friendly place to be. To laugh, to play, to be creative and imaginative are basic human needs. Some of our classrooms are not emotionally warm enough. I advocate that teachers share ideas and have staff Circle Times where they can experience the support and help of others, in order to understand the importance of maintaining the same ethos for their pupils. If a teacher is not heard or supported by their staff members, they will have no energy to give to the class. So, an emotionally safe school will have Circle Time for staff and pupils.

How can I get my current class to respond as well to Golden Time as previous classes have?

Q I have been using Golden Time in my classroom for several years now. It helps my children keep to the Golden Rules and gives us all something to look forward to at the end of the week. My current group of children, however, are not responding to it as I hoped they would. They do not seem to get excited about it, and this is lessening its effect as an incentive. Can you recommend anything? I am not sure where I'm going wrong with this group.

A Golden Time is only golden if you make it so. You must build it up into a celebration by your language, by everything. You have spent several years with Golden Time so it may be 'old hat' to you, but it is new for your current class. They need to know that it is special and that you value it highly. Take a few moments to think about how you sell Golden Time to the children. What sort of language do you use? What sort of priority do you give it? How do you make it special, a celebration?

Another possible source of problems could be the activities that are provided. It would be worth talking in a round with your class during Circle Time about what activities they value highly and find really exciting. Maybe what is on offer is somehow dated or tatty, or has lost its gilt-edged Golden Time charm? You can try everything from having special visitors to the classroom to using computers, doing cookery (quick things like icing a biscuit), to establishing special clubs or doing parachute games.

Once you have a list of what your children value most highly, you can work out if there is any money available in the budget, or maybe arrange some creative trips to jumble sales and car boot sales to buy new games, puzzles, dressing-up clothes or whatever else will help to put the sparkle back into Golden Time.

Remember that there may be resources within your school that you can use – play areas indoors or outside, the assembly hall, musical instruments, a parachute or computers. You can always vary the activities between individual, paired and whole-class fun.

And now some questions from newly qualified teachers.

Can Golden Time work as a system where the class earns points before gaining Golden Time?

Q In my class of Year 4 children, there are several who display behavioural problems, which results in disruptions for the rest of us and much time being wasted. I wanted to introduce Golden Time as an incentive, something for children to work towards. In this school, the children need to earn points during the week, and they know they must earn fifty class points before they can have their Golden Time on Friday afternoon. Although many of the children work towards this goal, several do not respond and quite often some children struggle to reach the fifty points needed. Can you suggest where I might be going wrong and what I could try to make this system work?

A You are certainly right to introduce an incentive system to help with the behaviour in your class, and I realise how much effort this takes. However, you will have more success if you eradicate the class earning-points system and tell the children that they will all automatically win the treat of Golden Time for keeping to the class Golden Rules (these must be in place first). This way each child will come in every Monday morning with a glow inside, knowing that they are trusted to keep the Golden Rules. The psychology that will work best is one of trust, not of earning points.

Golden Time will need to consist of special, new or exciting treats and activities to keep the power within the system. You then need to add to your system the knowledge that any child breaking one of the Golden Rules will lose five minutes of Golden Time. Only if a child loses all their Golden Time will you give them the opportunity to win back five minutes of Golden Time each time you negotiate a co-operative piece of behaviour. During their lost Golden Time, children sit observing a sand timer until they are allowed to come back to the class and join in with activities.

How can I convince other adults that Golden Time is a valuable use of time?

Q The headteacher at the school where I work is concerned about putting time aside for Golden Time – or playing, as he sees it. He is concerned that we will not have enough time for curriculum activities, and that the parents will see it as their children not receiving their entitlement of formal lesson time. I am keen to introduce Golden Time as I need help with behaviour management in my class. Can you offer any advice?

A You must explain to your headteacher that time is being wasted in class because of lack of structure for behaviour management and an effective sanctions and incentives policy. Why not ask your headteacher if you could run a pilot, using it for a term to see how well it works in your class? You could offer to talk it through at a staff meeting where all the staff can ask you questions. It would be much better if another teacher, preferably of an older or younger age group, could run a pilot alongside yours. You could share ideas and let the children carry out Golden Time activities with each other.

You could start by asking to be able to take fifteen or twenty minutes on a Friday afternoon. A letter could be sent to parents to tell them what you will be doing and why, and linking it to the Golden Rules. You could even invite them in for a Golden Time to see for themselves how the system works. Most parents are happy with what you decide will help with behaviour management, once they realise that there is a method in your system and that it is fair for their child. It will also help if they hear that the lost thirty minutes on a Friday afternoon are more than gained during the week. In fact, research has shown that teachers lose 20 per cent of teaching time if they do not have, and use, a clear, consistent and agreed incentives and sanctions system.

⑩

Case studies

When we wrote to teachers asking for any information they could share with us regarding how Golden Time operated in their schools, we received a wealth of wisdom in the post in reply. Amongst the replies, we were sent items like newsletters that went to parents, and individual accounts written specifically for us. Phone calls too followed fast and furious. It was a very exciting time. We decided to include a range of these accounts to inspire other schools to travel similar paths. They are not strictly case studies, but we like the rigour those words imply.

We are starting up a Quality Circle Time newsletter to carry on disseminating good practice. Nothing succeeds like success. So please, please, if you know that you have, through our model, adapted, developed or pioneered any exciting initiatives, send them in to the Circle Time e-mail address: circletime@jennymosley.co.uk

Case study 1

Golden Time *at Birley Spa Community Primary School, Sheffield*
Ian Read, SENCo

Catching the 'always' children
At the heart of our behaviour policy are a number of initiatives, which run consistently throughout our school and target, in particular, those children who always follow our school's Golden Rules.

Golden Time

Every child in our school starts each new week with an entitlement of thirty minutes' Golden Time on a Friday afternoon. They can lose it in blocks of five minutes if they break our Golden Rules. In Golden Time staff run a range of activities, which were chosen by the children. Children get to choose which activity they want to go to each week. Each school week ends on Friday afternoon with children taking part in Golden Time. In our index for inclusion survey, over 70 per cent of our children listed Golden Time in their top three favourite things about school.

Lunchtime Stars

Lunchtime Stars are a way of rewarding the children who, at lunchtime, are always helpful to our lunchtime staff, or who make a special effort. It is also a way of ensuring that lunchtimes end on a positive note back in the classroom.

After the lunchtime supervisor has fed back to the class teacher about lunchtime, four stickers are presented daily to children who have particularly impressed the supervisor. At the end of each week, four certificates are also given out to children who have stood out over the course of the week. These certificates are recorded and as children collect more they can earn spendable certificates and vouchers, which are presented in assembly.

Shining Stars

Shining Stars are children in our school who may stand out for doing that something extra or a little bit special. Any member of staff can give any child a Shining Star. The reasons for giving a Shining Star are explained as the child is given a certificate with a token on it. The child keeps the certificate, and the token is cut off and taken to the headteacher's office, where it is put in the Shining Star basket. Invariably the headteacher will ask what the Shining Star has been awarded for, and the child will sign their name with a gold pen in the Shining Star Book. Every month ten children's tokens are drawn out of the basket in assembly and these children go out with the headteacher for lunch.

All of these initiatives have become successfully established in school, and not only have they become a way of rewarding the children who always follow our Golden Rules, but they are also a way of 'capturing' other children who may not always follow the rules. The consistent implementation of these initiatives throughout the school over a number of years has helped to raise the standards of and expectations for behaviour in our school significantly.

Worry box

A worry box has been in place in our school for a number of years and is, as its name suggests, an outlet for children to voice their worries or concerns. We have two boxes, one in the infant area of the school and one in the junior area. Children can write a note and post it in the box. Our learning mentor checks the boxes daily, and she discreetly records and follows up any issues that are raised by a child. She will, with the child's permission, liaise with any appropriate people. What happens is monitored and followed up if any action is required.

Issues raised may range from relatively trivial school matters to incidents of bullying or upsetting issues outside school. The worry box is a way of reaching some children who may not otherwise feel able to access support in school and consequently may be unhappy in school for a whole variety of reasons. Part of its success lies in the fact that all incidents are dealt with sensitively, consistently and by the same person.

Behaviour Satellite Group

The Behaviour Satellite Group is simply a group of interested teachers who meet regularly to discuss and come up with solutions for dealing with issues of behaviour in school.

We have seven members of staff (almost a third of our teaching staff) involved in the group. The key principles that we operate under are that, wherever possible:

- children should be encouraged to manage their own behaviour;
- children should have ownership of initiatives that are set up;
- any initiatives that are set up should be applied consistently throughout the school.

We try to follow a cycle within which, as a group, we look at and suggest possible solutions to problems. These go to the headteacher and senior management team for approval. They will be presented at a staff meeting before being implemented throughout the school for a trial period. After half a term or so, they will be reviewed and evaluated at our next meeting. In this way it is hoped that whatever action we do take will have a lasting effect in the school.

Case study 2

Positive behaviour management *at Northwood School, Isle of Wight*
Vicki Johnson, Headteacher

Policy into practice
We start from the expectation that all the children will agree to keep the Golden Rules. The rules are clearly displayed throughout the school, in classes as well as in corridors. Parents are told what the rules are, either during a home visit or by reading the school brochure. A reminder of the rules is sent home in a newsletter to coincide with assembly themes on behaviour issues.

Managing classroom behaviour
The emphasis in the classroom is on praising the positive, without giving 'blanket praise'. We are aware of the need to ensure that the praise ratio is kept to at least 5:1. Each class has a selection of praise badges which give positive messages for a wide range of behaviours, such as 'I am a good reader', 'I am a good listener', 'I think hard', 'I am friendly' through to 'I am a cool dude'. (The last mentioned is particularly coveted.) The teachers rotate the badges and renew them to keep interest high. Teachers articulate what they like about what the child is doing, as opposed to saying what they dislike. Research in Nottingham showed that teachers praise work regularly, but omit to praise behaviour.

Key Stage 1 and 2 children are rewarded each week for keeping the Golden Rules with half an hour of Golden Time. Activities at this time are of the children's choosing and are negotiated at the beginning of the week. They can be anything from computer games to stories, games from home, Lego™ and so on. Children lose the right to some of their Golden Time only if they have been clearly warned and the choice of good or poor behaviour has been clearly explained. Each class has its own system of reminding children to keep the rules, and of displaying a warning to children who are in danger of losing Golden Time. It is seen as an important part of the practice that the ultimate sanction is kept for children who have made a deliberate choice to break the rules. Time out of Golden Time is meted out in five-minute chunks, depending upon the number of offences.

Each class has its own system for supplementing the Golden Rules. Reception, for example, has a pot in which children put marbles for 'marblous behaviour'. By the third term, the marbles are dropped into a marble run with a bell at the end of the last chute in order to keep the reward fresh and worthwhile. When the class has filled the pot, they bake a cake to share with each other.

Managing out-of-class behaviour

Meal supervisory assistants (MSAs) and classroom support workers shared training with staff when reviewing this policy, and meet with the headteacher on a regular basis to monitor its effectiveness. The school believes that every effort must be made to ensure that the values in the classroom are echoed in the playground. MSAs are seen as a very important part of the school team. They are encouraged to nominate children for the Golden Behaviour book, which is read out in Sharing Assembly on Friday mornings. Parents and volunteers often mingle with the children during lunch and break times. It is expected that support staff will always talk positively about the children in their care.

MSAs nominate children to sit at a special table as a reward for keeping the Golden Rules at lunchtime. Those nominated invite a friend to sit with them, and are allowed into the hall first.

It has been found that the difficult times have occurred most frequently when children are cramped onto the winter site. As a consequence much time and money has been spent on re-thinking this area.

The playground has been made into different zones:

1 The Millennium Trail.
2 The football zone.
3 Barry's bower.
4 Quiet area.
5 Craze of the week.

Each class uses the Millennium Trail in turn on a rota basis. There is a code of conduct for children using the apparatus. The football zone can be used only by children who wear a football rosette as a symbol of their right to play. They follow a special set of Football at Playtime Rules and have to attend a meeting to agree those rules before being allowed to wear a rosette. Children who misbehave lose the rosette, and are easily identifiable by MSAs and other adults.

Barry's bower has outdoor dressing-up clothes and props for children to use as role-play materials.

The quiet area has picnic tables and benches for children to use for drawing, their own board games, meeting together and so on.

The craze of the week is supplied by the school, and includes skipping ropes, cat's cradle, softballs, yo-yos, French skipping and shuttlecock games. All sets are rotated to ensure that there is renewed interest.

The MSAs are supported by a buddy scheme, which ensures that the children take responsibility for their school community. Children are invited to apply for the post of buddy and are interviewed before being given the job. All buddies are expected to serve for half a term before having their job reviewed. Four different children work each day, distinguished by an armband. They are given a job description and meet at half-termly intervals to discuss any difficulties. One of their main roles is to check the buddy stop, the place where any child may go if they are looking for a friend.

Case study 3

Golden Time *at Nyland School, Swindon*
P. Sunners, headteacher

We introduced Golden Time in September 1998. We are a special school for primary-aged children with social, emotional and behavioural difficulties. We use Golden Time to underpin our whole-school approach to behaviour, using the Golden Rules. We use Golden Time on a daily basis to reinforce appropriate behaviour and to facilitate a daily opportunity for pupils to make positive choices, which in many cases leads to positive interaction with others – an essential life skill.

Golden Rules are used to reinforce the privilege of Golden Time. Whole-school Circle Time assembly each Friday provides an opportunity to 'commune' as a whole school – to celebrate success and to offer an important opportunity for pupils to express their thoughts. This adheres to the principle of giving each child a voice.

We offer our children a twenty-minute daily Golden Time with a full range of activities, which include an opportunity for pupils to elect for a quiet time – a choice that facilitates emotional stability and calmness.

In addition to Golden Time, our school uses what is known as a Merit Award System, which leads to certificates, badges and medals based on a coherent system that the whole school understands.

We also use some gloriously simple prose in our whole-school documents. We chose texts based on an earthly spirituality to support 'grounding' children and staff, in both the simplicity and the richness of life. After all, the success of Circle Time, Golden Time and the Golden Rules depends on their simplicity.

Case Study 4

Golden Time *at Marion Richardson School, Stepney, London*
Justine Slaymaker, former class teacher

Golden Time was initiated within early years and Key Stage 1 as a result of the school SENCo attending a training course on the use of Circle Time and Golden Time to establish a positive behaviour-management strategy.

The programme was piloted in Year 1. The introduction of the Golden Rules, Circle Time and Golden Time quickly began to have an impact on children's behaviour across the three classes. Children from Year 1 became very proud of the fact that in their class they had 'Golden Time'. It also had an effect on attendance, with Wednesday (Circle Time and Golden Time choices) and Friday (Golden Time) becoming 100 per cent attendance days. The experience of the Year 1 teachers and their good practice was shared with the early years and Year 2 classes.

All classrooms used the sun, sun and cloud, and grey cloud model with name pegs. All classrooms developed Golden Time focus areas where the Golden Rules were prominently displayed alongside any work produced during Circle Time. Within the Golden Time display space, teachers included wipe-off boards which clearly indicated activities that children had selected for Golden Time. Golden Time activity choices were made every Wednesday following Circle Time. This ensured that the children were regularly reminded that Golden Time was directly related to keeping the Golden Rules.

Initiatives that developed as a result of establishing the Golden Rules:

- Class Golden Books – teachers wrote the names of children in their classes and the Golden Rule they had practised in a gold-bound book. The children's names were shared with visitors to the class and parents, along with the rule they were practising.

- Golden cards issued at playtime to value the Golden Rules remembered by children.

- 'Tell me a good tale' – a five-minute session following playtime in which children were encouraged to describe something good that happened during play. Teachers linked this to the Golden Rules.

Activities for Golden Time

Teachers responded to children's requests for particular activities. Often five group activities were set up, on the understanding that one activity would demand teacher support. I developed a Golden Time Box in which templates and activities were stored. Activities were often derived from children's experiences of different areas of the curriculum. This was a great opportunity to extend and consolidate their learning. Here are some examples:

1 Children often selected activities in response to books read (both fiction and non-fiction):
   - Making character masks.
   - Making crafts from non-fiction activity books.
   - Making story settings – spooky houses.
   - Making school and lunch registers.
   - Revisiting CD-ROMs and having a more sustained experience.
   - Reading comics.

2 Activities in response to art and design and technology:
   - Still-life sketching – using a range of drawing media.
   - Collage.
   - Cutting and sticking – making cards and stationery.
   - Model making – Play-Doh® and construction kits.
   - Cooking – icing biscuits, making coconut ice or instant puddings set in cake cases.
   - Making books.

3 Activities in response to science:
- – Planting seeds.
- – Making egg and cress heads.

Some activities were purely in response to children's ideas and these were never in short supply. Examples include these:

- Making fairy wings, wands, head-dresses.
- Making dragon or wizard wings and wands.
- Jigsaws and board games.
- Sand and water trays.
- Dressing up.
- Playing instruments.
- Small-world play – cars and road maps, dinosaurs, Playmobil, teddy bears' picnic.

Case study 5

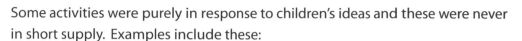

Allanton Primary School, Shotts, in North Lanarkshire, where
Golden Time is a key strategy in schools
Aileen Ronald, Headteacher

Positive behaviour management through Golden Time

I started as a new headteacher in Allanton in 1999. Some teachers had already attended Circle Time courses and found it extremely worthwhile to do with their classes. Their enthusiasm for Circle Time spread through discussion in the staffroom, resulting in all staff wanting to be trained in Circle Time, which was then actioned over the course of the session.

About this time we heard about Golden Time and that North Lanarkshire Council were trying to encourage their schools to use this as a positive behaviour strategy.

We decided to contact Margo Hackland, an adviser for North Lanarkshire Council, to ask how we could learn more about Golden Time. She organised an in-service training day for us (this included clerical and janitorial staff) with another local school. This training day was led by none other than Jenny Mosley, with support from Margo Hackland.

Before Golden Time was introduced, the ethos in the school was good, with various reward systems in place both in school and class, and these appeared to work. On hearing about Golden Time, however, we felt that the children who always tried to give of their best would be rewarded on a weekly basis and would never be overlooked, which can sometimes be the case, no matter how hard you try.

We worked in partnership with all the parents, informing them of our decision regarding Golden Time and updating them about Golden Time via our monthly newsletter. We organised a parents' evening with Margo Hackland to allow those interested to ask questions. All the parents who attended thought that Golden Time was a good idea.

A Golden Time leaflet was designed, and each class made up their own class rules, which were incorporated into the leaflet along with the Golden Rules. Parents were asked to sign a partnership agreement to support us in this initiative, and all the parents agreed.

The children were informed about Golden Time via our weekly school assembly and again in each class both within, and outside, Circle Time. The pupils were shown the games that had been purchased for Golden Time in assembly.

A working party was formed to develop a whole-school approach to Golden Time and Circle Time. Books were purchased, along with Golden Time posters illustrating the Golden Time rules for each class, and resources were purchased to make Golden Time more interesting and exciting. A special display area was set up with photographs to allow the whole school to select their chosen activity on a Friday afternoon. All staff were involved, and everyone was aware of the ethos.

What is special about Golden Time in our school is that everyone works as part of a team. It is a partnership. We have developed Golden Time over the years to suit us, and the whole team has been involved in the decision-making processes.

Among our refinements of the system, we decided not to use a large display board, and each class is responsible for organising their own activities. We also organised personnel in the school to offer their services on a Friday afternoon to take various Golden Time activities – that is, classroom assistants, SEN auxiliary staff and the headteacher. We also arranged for parent helpers to come in to help at this time.

We decided to have a Golden Table on Friday lunchtimes, and started with a special tablecloth. Over the years our School Council have developed this idea with suggestions from the pupils. We have added flowers to the table, and orange juice. Last year we ran a competition to design table mats. Every Friday, at our weekly assembly, four pupils who have been kind and caring to others are chosen to sit at this table at lunchtime. Their names are shown on a large display in our main hall, and these children each choose a friend to join them at the table. In future, we intend to develop a small certificate which pupils will take home to let their parents know about their reward.

We extended Golden Time into our playground by trying to make it a more fun and interesting place to be. We added playground games and established a picnic garden area, and we dotted benches about the playground. We introduced warning cards some time ago, but we tend not to use these. This year we purchased a Friendship Stop and baseball caps for Playground Friends, and also a plaque displaying five useful playground rules for a happy playground. Our local authority adviser is going to share ideas about how we can develop our playground, focusing on positive behaviour.

We issue the Golden Time booklet to all our parents at the start of every year and ask them all to sign the partnership agreement. We also discuss Golden Time with our new parents. The Golden Rules are displayed on a board in our Nursery class, and a booklet is sent to the Nursery parents. Although the children do not participate in Golden Time activities at this stage, they do participate in Circle Time. I think in this way Golden Time becomes a way of life and all the children are immersed in the rules and rewards. It works for us and we aim to continue with Golden Time and develop it over the years to keep it fresh and interesting.

The staff, who were super anyway and always treated the pupils with respect, like Golden Time because they can reward all of their pupils. The pupils who work, and may sometimes be overlooked, get to see the benefits of continuing with their hard work and good behaviour. It means for me as a manager that I can say to supply teachers, 'This is our policy and this works – please use it.' I make it clear that there is no need to be harsh with the children or issue unrealistic punishments. This sometimes works, which I think is a big compliment to our staff, who make it work through their effort and by being conscientious.

Informing governors, parents and carers about Golden Time and your positive behaviour-management policy

Behavioural-policy information that schools provide for parents

We have found increasingly that schools are sharing their good practice with parents. This has many advantages; parents understand how your incentives system and the various stages of your policy work, and they have the opportunity of supporting your activities, by being able to talk to their child about Golden Time with knowledge and understanding. Some parents are able to help by raising funds for Golden Time equipment, or by donating time and skills by coming in to help with the clubs.

Below are some encouraging letters and explanations from schools who are reaching out to their parents. In Appendix 1 (page 160), we provide a skeleton letter that may help you to structure your own explanation for parents about Golden Time.

Northwood School, Isle of Wight

Excerpt from a parent newsletter

October 1st 1999

- Is it my imagination or is it pouring with rain just as the children arrive, and then just as they go home? Feel free to come in and shelter wherever you can.
- You may have heard your child talk about our new Golden Rules. We have decided that, in order to set clearer 'boundaries' for everyone, it might be helpful to have some precise 'dos and don'ts' which we have put around the school, and which I have reproduced here for your information. Each class will be talking about them, and reviewing them in Circle Time. There is also a straightforward system of warnings and sanctions should it be necessary, although our overall strategy is to 'catch the children being good'.

DO	DON'T
We are gentle	We don't hurt anybody
We are kind and gentle	We don't hurt people's feelings
We are honest	We don't cover up the truth
We work hard	We don't waste time
We look after property	We don't waste or damage things
We listen to people	We don't interrupt

- I am very grateful to the kind children who have given up one playtime per week to become a playground buddy. All the applicants had to apply for the post, and we were thrilled with the response. We have a rota that will change at half-term to allow all those who were successful at their 'interview' to have a turn.

King's Furlong Infants School, Basingstoke

Letter to parents on the Internet

17th September 2001

Dear Parents

A warm welcome back to all parents and children, especially our new arrivals in the Reception classes and Nursery. The children all look very smart in their school uniform; our school shop is open from 9 to 9.15 a.m. each day, staffed by Mrs Smyth.

Golden Rules, Golden Time and Golden Post-box

As we start the new year may I remind you of our very successful behaviour and reward system based on 'King's Furlong Golden Rules'.

The children are familiar with these at all times of the school day and we would appreciate your support in discussing these with them. The children work towards being rewarded every Friday with 'Golden Time', where they have half an hour of specially chosen activities. Each week two children from each class are invited to a special 'Golden Tea Party' with Mrs Freshwater when their names are entered in a special Golden Book. At the end of each half-term, children who have achieved full 'Golden Time' every week receive a 'Golden Certificate'.

The 'Golden Post-box' is sited in the Jubilee Room and we ask all staff and parents, grandparents, childminders and so on to nominate a child for a particular special achievement (i.e. being kind, sharing, thoughtful actions); this can be at school or at home.

Please put the child's name and class and your reasons on a piece of paper and post in the box. (Note that these nominations are for very special achievements.) These children are celebrated at a 'Golden Moments' assembly on Mondays: their names are entered in the special 'Golden Book'. If you require any further information, please see your child's teacher.

➡

Special event: Mrs Freshwater's Golden Tea Party Week!

We are organising a tea party week from 1st to 5th October to which every child will be invited. Don't worry if your child isn't in full-time yet: he/she will still receive an invitation. This will be an exciting fund raising event to help young people with disabilities who attend the Lord Mayor Treloar School and College near Alton.

Your child will be receiving a special invitation to this event and will be asked to wear something 'golden' for the party (e.g. hat, hairband, belt . . . be as creative as you like!). The fee for joining this event will be £1. This is a golden opportunity for us to reflect and support those children with very special needs who attend this Hampshire school.

Golden Time at Kinson School, Bournemouth

Investors in People 2003, School Achievement Award

The vast majority of the children at Kinson School are well behaved all of the time.

At Kinson, the school has adopted a 'Golden Time' approach to reward good behaviour. Each week children have the right to thirty minutes of 'Golden Time'. During the week, each time a child breaks the Golden Rules they lose five minutes. The children can agree to earn back their time by following the Golden Rules. During 'Golden Time' the children who have lost some time watch the other children enjoying themselves with their friends. Many activities have been bought by funds raised by the PFA. Visit www.kinson.bournemouth.sch.uk for further details.

Positive behaviour at Westfield First School, Berkhampstead, Hertfordshire

Good behaviour is highly valued at Westfield, and we have an extensive list of rewards and sanctions to encourage this positively for each age group. Rewards include stickers, merit marks, headteacher certificates and table points.

Golden Time

This special time on each Friday afternoon is earned by the children when they behave well in class, and do not waste valuable teaching and learning time by disrupting the class. During Golden Time the children may choose between several activities and games, and sometimes share games brought in from home.

Loss of Golden Time is one of the sanctions we use when pupils choose not to behave well.

When pupils choose not to behave well, they are fully aware of the sanctions we have in place. The first step is a warning, then if the behaviour continues the child may be sent to the time-out table for a set period. At this table, the child will have to write about or draw a picture relating to the reason they were sent there, and how they could make the situation better. More serious sanctions include loss of a set period of playtime, a reduction of their 'Golden Time', letters to the child's parents and, in rare cases, short-term exclusions.

For further details see www.westfieldfirst.herts.sch.uk

Golden Time at Sacred Heart Catholic Primary School, Coventry

Where God's Holy People
Pray, reflect, learn,
And grow to mirror the love of Jesus

We are proud of our school ethos.
Visitors to the school regularly comment upon the warm welcome and friendly, caring atmosphere they experience. We continually seek to improve and develop the good behaviour of the children because we firmly believe that if children behave well they are happy, and if they are happy they will learn.

At the heart of our discipline policy are six rules that are rooted in Gospel values – a clear guide for Christian living and effective citizenship.

If a child follows our six Golden Rules, they automatically enjoy Golden Time on a Friday. On a Monday, each child signs up for an activity during Golden Time, for example disco, listening to a story tape, plasticine, watching a video. If, however, they do not follow the rules, they may forfeit some of their time in five-minute intervals. Once their forfeited time is up, they may go to their chosen activity.

For more details on our Golden Time activities visit
www.sacredheart.coventry.sch.uk

Promoting positive behaviour at Ashley Road Primary School, Aberdeen

Golden Time procedures

Within the classroom

- Establish the Golden Rules.
- Introduce the privilege of Golden Time for those who adhere to the rules.
- Golden Time should be special to encourage the children to be self-disciplined. Find out what the children would like included in Golden Time.
- Wherever possible, keep a regular slot for Golden Time. This allows the children to know what they are aiming for.

Breaking rules

- An instant loss of ten minutes' Golden Time.
- The child is sent to a member of the management team.
- A record is kept.
- Parents to be involved, when appropriate, by standard letter or personal contact.

Promoting positive behaviour

- Certificates awarded on a four-weekly basis.
- Certificates are counted and a 'Class of the Month' trophy is presented at assembly and fixed to the classroom door. There will be three trophies: Infant, Middle and Upper.
- At the end of the session, special certificates are awarded to those who have been in the sunshine all of the time.

12 Closing thoughts

Well, folks, we have shared with you the insights learnt from developing the model over many years. If you have made it this far through the book, well done. You can have your own Golden Time; you really deserve it! It is very easy, when time and energy are in constant demand, to short-cut areas in our work and personal lives in an attempt to make more time and energy for other areas. Some extra investments of time and energy will return to you more time and energy than you initially expended. Stephen Covey (1990) describes this as 'sharpening the saw'. We love this metaphor of encouraging you to spend time doing something (sharpening a saw), that will make the actual work (cutting down a tree) quicker, easier and less demanding. Sharpening the senses through devising joyful times for yourself will really help you to see the wood for the trees and to connect again with what a privilege it is to work with children.

This is how we see Golden Time. We hope that the effort that you expend in lovingly setting it up and making it exciting for the children will return to you after a shortish period of investment. If the children are happier, you will feel happier.

The other 'saw sharpening' that we always recommend, here at the consultancy, is to take care of yourself and each other. This means taking a few moments out when you need it; stopping to ask a colleague how they are; and taking enough time for your own personal interests, relaxation, family life and whatever nurtures you best.

We would love to have anecdotes of your own experiences of setting up or using Golden Time, or about any other Golden initiatives – ones from this book or ones creatively designed by you. Sharing our best practices will make successful strategies available to all, and our schools will become better places for learning and more caring environments in which to thrive.

Teaching is all about being courageous. Courage needs to be fuelled by energy, and energy is fuelled by golden moments.

Best wishes from us all – and please keep in touch.

1

Photocopiable resources

The following are photocopiable resources that have been developed for schools, or for use with parents or in training days. You are more than welcome to adapt or develop these yourself. To safeguard the integrity of the model, though, if you do decide to adapt any of these, please put 'Copyright QCT, Mosley, J.' at the bottom.

Golden Rules

We are gentle — We don't hurt others

We are kind and helpful — We don't hurt anybody's feelings

We listen — We don't interrupt

We are honest — We don't cover up the truth

We work hard — We don't waste our own or others' time

We look after property — We don't waste or damage things

I agree to support the Golden Rules ....
Parent/carer

Golden Time Activity List

Activity	Week	Week	Week	Week	Week	Week

Key Stage 2

Warning cards

Key Stage 1

WARNING

Name ....

WARNING

Name ....

WARNING

Name ....

WARNING

Name ....

Permission to Photocopy

Loss of Golden Time Chart

Name	5 mins.	10 mins.	15 mins.	20 mins.	25 mins.	30 mins.

For week ending ....

Earning Back Golden Time Contract

I agree to ....

.... (target)

in order to earn back .... minutes of Golden Time.

Signed .... Pupil

Signed .... Teacher

Earning Back Golden Time Contract

I agree to ....

.... (target)

in order to earn back .... minutes of Golden Time.

Signed .... Pupil

Signed .... Teacher

Golden Time Certificate

Congratulations

You have kept the Golden Rules.

We are gentle 😊 We don't hurt others

We are kind and helpful 😊 We don't hurt anybody's feelings

We listen 😊 We don't interrupt

We are honest 😊 We don't cover up the truth

We work hard 😊 We don't waste our own or others' time

We look after property 😊 We don't waste or damage things

Signed ....

Class Team Honours Certificate

We are really pleased to award

....

a class team honours
for

....

Signed ....

Golden Coins

Special Award

Well done

....

for earning .... Golden Coins

Signed ....

Tiny Achievable Tickable Targets instructions

Children beyond the normal motivational procedures such as your incentive and Golden Time systems will need to move onto the TATTs strategy. This involves letting go of the idea that this child can keep to the Golden Rules all the time. You need to negotiate with them specific times (using sand timers) during which they keep the Golden Rules for short periods. If the child reaches this target they will have a star/dot put into an appropriate box. You will agree tiny, easy targets at first which can be more challenging as each is reached. The secret of success lies in the agreed privilege which will accompany reaching the target. It is best when the child has a self-esteem reward, for example helping in another class/helping the caretaker. It is also best if you choose a different child from the class to accompany them each day as this encourages the others to support the child. Sometimes the most appropriate reward is a class certificate signed by all the children.

Tiny Achievable Tickable Targets

	Before play	Playtime	After play	Lunchtime	Afternoon
Monday					
Tuesday					
Wednesday					
Thursday					
Friday					

My target is to get .... stickers each day.

If I achieve my target I can ....

Signed ....   Signed ....

               Pupil   Teacher

Tiny Achievable Tickable Targets

	Before play	Playtime	After play	Lunchtime	Afternoon
Monday					
Tuesday					
Wednesday					
Thursday					
Friday					

My target is to get .... stickers each day.

If I achieve my target I can ....

Signed ....   Signed ....

               Pupil   Teacher

Lunchtime Invitation

Dear ....

Because you have kept the Golden Rules in the Dining Hall, you are invited to sit at our special table next week. Please bring a guest.

Signed .... Lunchtime Supervisor

Lunchtime Invitation

Dear ....

Because you have kept the Golden Rules in the Dining Hall, you are invited to sit at our special table next week. Please bring a guest.

Signed .... Lunchtime Supervisor

Permission to Photocopy

Lunchtime Congratulations

Name ....

You were kind to others.

You kept the lunchtime rules.

You played well with other children.

You kept calm.

You stood quietly and patiently in line.

Signed ....
Lunchtime Supervisor

Lunchtime Congratulations

Name ....

You were kind to others.

You kept the lunchtime rules.

You played well with other children.

You kept calm.

You stood quietly and patiently in line.

Signed ....
Lunchtime Supervisor

Sample Golden Time information letter

Here is an example of the type of letter primary schools have written to parents and carers. It is vital that, at every stage of your whole-school behaviour policy, you inform them about what you are planning to do and give them an opportunity to have their say. We have discovered that in schools that have rushed the process and omitted to consult parents, there is far more likely to be backlash: 'What do you mean, my kid is sitting watching a sand timer?', 'What a waste of time' – and before you know it, the discussions are too heated for understanding to take place.

The following example would need to be personalised with details and anecdotes from your own school.

Dear Parent or Carer

We are writing to tell you about our exciting new positive behaviour policy. Many of the children at our school are well behaved for most of the time. However, we feel we need to provide even clearer guidelines and boundaries to support each child in making the right decisions when choosing how they behave. As a result of talking with the children, we are introducing our new Golden Rules, which are as follows:

We are gentle	We don't hurt others
We are kind and helpful	We don't hurt anybody's feelings
We listen	We don't interrupt
We are honest	We don't cover up the truth
We work hard	We don't waste our own or others' time
We look after property	We don't waste or damage things

These are now our moral values. They will be displayed outside and inside. There are other sets of rules, like our rules for the dining areas and for the classroom, but these are routines for specific areas. The Golden Rules will remain the same.

To reward the children for keeping the Golden Rules all week, we shall be starting Golden Time on Friday afternoons (or as a shorter daily event for early years and early Key Stage 1). This will be a special session where all the children who have kept the Golden Rules all week (or all day) will

---

be able to choose an exciting activity to participate in, and we shall all celebrate together. We shall inform you at a later date about any activities with which we might need volunteer help. I am sure your child will update you about the new activities, and we look forward to inviting you in to see how they work at a later date.

Children who break any of the rules will be given a visual warning, and if they continue to choose to break a rule, they will lose five minutes of Golden Time (only 1 minute in early years and early Key Stage 1).

We shall discuss what happens with all the children regularly so that they fully understand how Golden Time works, and we shall support the children in trying to follow the Golden Rules so that losing Golden Time is not a common event.

If you have any queries, comments or offers of help, please do contact us.

Thank you in advance for your co-operation with this.

Golden Time within the context of the Primary National Strategy

How does Golden Time mesh with the current guidance documents?

Excellence and Enjoyment (DfES, 2003b) heralds a move towards addressing the need of children to enjoy their lessons and their learning environment, as well as the teaching and learning of positive behaviour.

o Primary schools have a critical role in teaching children positive behaviour, and must be supported in building strong approaches to behaviour into the way they teach and into the ethos of the school.

o Primary school staff rate training in how to promote positive behaviour as one of their highest priority needs.

o Promoting positive behaviour needs to cover teaching positive behaviour for all children, as well as working with children who show early signs of behaviour and attendance problems.

o Teaching positive behaviour for all children means supporting good behaviour as part of the way children are taught.

DfES (2003b)

Interestingly, this paper recognises the importance that primary schools play in teaching positive behaviour to children, and it even recognises the distinction between supporting good behaviour and teaching positive behaviour, which is a subtlety that is sometimes overlooked. Using the Golden Rules as a framework to teach positive behaviour, and Golden Time to celebrate rule keeping and reward the positive behaviour, addresses this. When both Golden Time and the Golden Rules are promoted and used, then positive behaviour is being taught as well as reinforced and rewarded.

Golden Time within the context of the National Curriculum

Most of us want at least some of our children to behave in better ways, and want the confidence and self-esteem of many of our children to be raised. Several of the current government strategies point in this general direction. The real nub of the matter is that, in order for them to want to improve their behaviour in school, young children need an incentive to work towards. Teachers carry out all sorts of activities on a shoestring budget, and are often asked to provide all manner of resources throughout the course of a year – audio; visual; things to taste, smell, create, disassemble, assemble and communicate with. In which other profession do you see staff resourcing their work materials at jumble sales or car boot sales, or collecting shiny paper and cartons? This is all done in the name of teaching and the creation of stimulating learning experiences.

When we are asked to address the various behaviours that are found in our classrooms, and to teach positive behaviour actively, we need real incentives so that children will sit up and listen, knowing that we mean business. We cannot ask teachers to improve the behaviour of pupils in their class without a proper, workable, achievable, affordable incentives system. Golden Time can provide such an incentive, but it needs a little bit of planning, some resourcing and the co-operation of other adults in the classroom. It will also need a mini-marketing strategy to sell the idea to the children. It needs to be talked about enthusiastically and with a sparkle in the eye. And it will reap rewards for you as well as the children, helping to free up teaching and learning time.

The National Curriculum Handbook for Primary Teachers in England

Excerpts from the National Curriculum for Key Stage 1

Developing confidence and responsibility and making the most of their abilities

Pupils should be taught:

a) to recognise what they like and dislike, what is fair and unfair, and what is right and wrong

Preparing to play an active role as citizens

Pupils should be taught:

c) to recognise choices they can make, and recognise the difference between right and wrong

d) to agree and follow rules for their group and classroom, and understand how rules help them

Developing a healthy, safer lifestyle

Pupils should be taught:

a) how to make simple choices that improve their health and well-being

Developing good relationships and respecting the differences between people

Pupils should be taught:

a) to recognise how their behaviour affects other people

b) to listen to other people, and play and work cooperatively

During the key stage, pupils should be taught the **Knowledge, skills and understanding** through opportunities to:

a) take and share responsibility [for example, for their own behaviour; by helping to make classroom rules and following them; by looking after pets well]

b) feel positive about themselves [for example, by having their achievements recognised and by being given positive feedback about themselves]

d) make real choices [for example, between healthy options in school meals, what to watch on television, what games to play, how to spend and save money sensibly]

f) develop relationships through work and play [for example, by sharing equipment with other pupils or their friends in a group task]

DfEE (1999)

At Key Stage 1, the words 'preparing', 'developing' and 'opportunities' spring up in relation to the choices children learn to make regarding their own behaviour and managing themselves. This is a key aspect of Golden Time, as children are continually presented with the idea that their behaviour is their choice. If they keep to the Golden Rules, they have the choice of real activities to enjoy during Golden Time. If they choose to misbehave, break one of the Golden Rules and lose Golden Time, they will be provided with opportunities to win back their time. It is all about choice, and about developing their understanding of how the choices they make affect their opportunities and enjoyment.

The fact that children are asked to sign up for activities for Golden Time is a good opportunity for making, and sticking to, real choices, and for thinking things through before deciding finally. It represents real preparation for the many decisions they will be asked to make as an older primary-aged child and as a teenager.

> *One school we asked said that, although the children enjoyed the range of activities offered during Golden Time, the thing they liked best was that they were offered a choice. The opportunity to choose was the reward for them.*

Excerpts from the National Curriculum for Key Stage 2

Developing confidence and responsibility and making the most of their abilities

Pupils should be taught:

b) to recognise their worth as individuals by identifying positive things about themselves and their achievements, seeing their mistakes, making amends and setting personal goals

Preparing to play an active roles as citizens

Pupils should be taught:

b) why and how rules and laws are made and enforced, why different rules are needed in different situations and how to take part in making and changing rules

d) that there are different kinds of responsibilities, rights and duties at home, at school and in the community, and that these can sometimes conflict with each other

Developing good relationships and respecting the differences between people

Pupils should be taught:

a) that their actions affect themselves and others, to care about other people's feelings and to try to see things from their points of view

During the key stage, pupils should be taught the **Knowledge, skills and understanding** through opportunities to:

b) feel positive about themselves [for example, by producing personal diaries, profiles and portfolios of achievements; by having opportunities to show what they can do and how much responsibility they can take]

d) make real choices and decisions [for example, about issues affecting their health and well-being such as smoking; on the use of scarce resources; how to spend money, including pocket money and contributions to charities]

f) develop relationships through work and play [for example, taking part in activities with groups that have particular needs, such as children with special needs and the elderly; communicating with children in other countries by satellite, e-mail or letters]

DfEE (1999)

Like the targets for Key Stage 1, many of the Key Stage 2 objectives are geared towards personal development, relationships and choice making, as well as towards taking responsibility and abiding by rules. Once again, using Golden Time provides children with regular opportunities to learn how to choose behaviours appropriate to the situations they find themselves in. It also teaches them about relationship patterns with adults and other children, and making real choices that will affect them in ways that they will notice. All day children are asked to make choices and think in terms of lessons and learning, but many choices cover theoretical work or theoretical applications, and there are fewer opportunities to carry out practical applications. With much of the school day being taken up with academic pursuits, the Golden Rules – Golden Time partnership provides on-going opportunities to manage the Key Stage 2 PSHE targets during the week.

Appendix

(4)

Sources

References

Bandura, A. (1977) *Social Learning Theory*. London: Prentice Hall Inc.

Covey, S. (1990) *The Seven Habits of Highly Effective People*. London: Simon and Schuster UK Ltd

DfEE (1999) *The National Curriculum. Handbook for Primary Schools*. London: DfEE and QCA

DfEE (2001) *Promoting Children's Mental Health within Early Years and School Settings*. Nottingham: DfEE Publications

DfES (2003a) *Developing Children's Social, Emotional and Behavioural Skills: A Whole-curriculum Approach*. Nottingham: DfES Publications

DfES (2003b) *Excellence and Enjoyment. A Strategy for Primary Schools*. Nottingham: DfES Publications

Goleman, D. (1996) *Emotional Intelligence. Why it can matter more than IQ*. London: Bloomsbury

Maslow, A. (1968) *Towards a Psychology of Being*. New York: Van Nostrand Reinhold

HMIE (2004) *Personal Support for Pupils in Scottish Schools* (available online)

Mosley, J. (1989) *All Round Success*. Trowbridge: Wiltshire Local Education Authority

Mosley, J. (1993) *Turn Your School Round*. Cambridge: LDA

Mosley, J. (1996) *Quality Circle Time*. Cambridge: LDA

Mosley, J. (1998) *More Quality Circle Time*. Cambridge: LDA

Mosley, J. (2001) *Photocopiable Materials for use with the Jenny Mosley Quality Circle Time Model.* Trowbridge: Positive Press Ltd

Mosley, J. and Thorp, G. (2002) *All Year Round.* Cambridge: LDA

Sharp, P. (2001) *Nurturing Emotional Literacy. A Practical Guide for Teachers, Parents and those in the Caring Professions.* London: David Fulton Publishers Ltd

Taylor, M. (2003) *Going Round in Circles. Implementing and Learning from Circle Time.* Slough: NFER Publications

Useful organisations

All Round Success (Registered Charity no. 1064740)

28a Gloucester Road, Trowbridge, Wiltshire BA14 0AA
Tel: 01225 767157; Fax: 01225 755631

Anti-bullying Network

Moray House School of Education, University of Edinburgh, Holyrood Road, Edinburgh EH8 8AQ
Tel: 0131 651 6100; Fax: 0131 651 6088; www.antibullying.net

Antidote

3rd Floor, Cityside House, 40 Alder Street, Aldgate, London E1 1EE
Tel: 020 7247 3355; Fax: 020 7247 7992; www.antidote.org.uk

Campaign For Learning

Head Office Address: Campaign for Learning, 19 Buckingham Street, London WC2N 6EF
Tel: 020 7930 1111; Fax: 020 7930 1551; www.campaign-for-learning.org.uk

Centre for Child Mental Health

2–18 Britannia Row, London N1 8PA
Tel: 020 7354 2913; www.childmentalhealthcentre.org

Jenny Mosley Consultancies and Positive Press

28a Gloucester Road, Trowbridge, Wiltshire BA14 0AA
Tel: 01225 767157; Fax: 01225 755631; www.circle-time.co.uk

Nurture Groups

Institute of Education, University of London, 20 Bedford Way, London WC1H 0AL
Tel: 020 7612 6589/91; Fax: 020 7612 6600; www.nurturegroups.org

Young Minds

102–108 Clerkenwell Road, London EC1M 5SA
Tel: 020 7336 8445; Fax: 020 7336 8446; www.youngminds.org.uk

Quality Circle Time books and resources

Goldthorpe, M. (1998) *Effective IEPs through Circle Time.* Cambridge: LDA

Goldthorpe, M. (1998) *Poems for Circle Time and Literacy Hour.* Cambridge: LDA

Goldthorpe, M. and Nutt, L. (2005) *Assemblies to Teach Golden Rules* (New Edition). Cambridge: LDA

Luck, D. and Doyle, J. (2004) *We are Gentle . . . We Don't Hurt Others.* Trowbridge: Positive Press Ltd

Luck, D. and Doyle, J. (2004) *We are Honest . . . We Don't Cover up the Truth.* Trowbridge: Positive Press Ltd

Luck, D. and Doyle, J. (2004) *We are Kind and Helpful . . . We Don't Hurt Anybody's Feelings.* Trowbridge: Positive Press Ltd

Luck, D. and Doyle, J. (2004) *We Listen . . . We Don't Interrupt.* Trowbridge: Positive Press Ltd

Mosley, J. (1989) *All Round Success.* Trowbridge: Wiltshire Local Education Authority

Mosley, J. (1993) *Turn Your School Round.* Cambridge: LDA

Mosley, J. (1996) *Quality Circle Time.* Cambridge: LDA

Mosley, J. (1998) *More Quality Circle Time.* Cambridge: LDA

Mosley, J. (2001) *Photocopiable Materials for use with the Jenny Mosley Quality Circle Time Model.* Trowbridge: Positive Press

Mosley, J. and Gillibrand, E. (2001) *Personal Power. How to fulfil your Private and Professional Life.* Trowbridge: Positive Press

Mosley, J. and Sonnet, H. (2001) *Here we Go Round. Quality Circle Time for 3–5 Year Olds.* Trowbridge: Positive Press

Mosley, J. and Sonnet, H. (2002) *101 Games for Self-Esteem.* Cambridge: LDA

Mosley, J. and Sonnet, H. (2002) *101 Games for Social Skills.* Cambridge: LDA

Mosley, J. and Sonnet, H. (2002) *Making Waves.* Cambridge: LDA

Mosley, J. and Sonnet, H. (2003) *Clapping Games. Whole Brain Workout for Lively Children.* Trowbridge: Positive Press

Mosley, J. and Sonnet, H. (2003) *More Clapping Games. Whole Brain Workout for Lively Children.* Trowbridge: Positive Press

Mosley, J. and Thorp, G. (2002) *All Year Round.* Cambridge: LDA

Mosley, J. and Thorp, G. (2002) *Playground Games.* Cambridge: LDA

Mosley, J. and Thorp, G. (2002) *Playground Notelets.* Cambridge: LDA

Mosley, J. (1996) *Class Reward Sheets.* Cambridge: LDA

Mosley, J. (1996) *Responsibility Badges.* Cambridge: LDA

Mosley, J. (2000) *Quality Circle Time in Action.* Cambridge: LDA

Mosley, J. (2000) *Quality Circle Time Kit.* Cambridge: LDA

Mosley, J. (2004) *Reward Certificates.* Cambridge: LDA

Mosley, J. (2004) *Stickers.* Cambridge: LDA

Mosley, J. (2005) *Golden Rules Posters.* Cambridge: LDA

For information about the full range of Jenny Mosley's books and resources, please contact LDA Customer Services on 0845 120 4776 or visit our website at www.LDAlearning.com

Training available from Jenny Mosley Consultancies

Developing the Quality Circle Time model

Jenny Mosley's Whole School Quality Circle Time model is now well established and welcomed by thousands of schools throughout the UK. In recent years it has been adopted in many countries. The ease with which the model has been transferred to different cultures is an indication of the universal psychology underpinning the method.

Our team of accredited trainers

Jenny has drawn together a number of highly experienced, well-qualified consultants whose wide-ranging skills cover many areas within education. Evaluations and letters of testimony are available upon request. To become a 'Jenny Mosley consultant' you follow a one-to-two-year programme of training, action research, shadowing and on-going mentoring and supervision.

Our courses are for all educators – encompassing headteachers, teachers, learning mentors, behaviour support teams, teaching assistants, educational psychologists, admin support teams and many others.

Headteachers and Ofsted reports have commented that the Quality Circle Time model helps schools work towards their policies for the following:

o emotional literacy;
o citizenship;
o anti-bullying;
o racial harmony;
o speaking and listening;
o staff health and well-being;

o PSHE;
o positive behaviour;
o drugs;
o RE;
o creativity;
o communication.

Create happier lunchtimes and playtimes – a whole-school approach

If a child is unhappy at lunchtime, they are unhappy at school. This training day:

o helps the whole school promote a positive lunchtime policy;

o re-energises the buddy system, improves wet play and dining halls;

o supports all the adults and children in engaging in creative play.

A closure day – achieving excellence through valuing individuals; sharing the vision

The day will help you to:

o raise the self-esteem and morale of adults and children;

o re-evaluate your current listening systems, including Circle Time, Golden Rules, incentives and sanctions, lunchtime and children 'beyond' policies;

o draw all the adults together towards a shared vision of a happy and respectful team.

Children 'beyond' – pupils who challenge our hearts, minds and bodies!

This course looks at children whose emotional and behavioural needs cannot be met by the usual motivational strategies. During this day we help you to:

o assess your current positive behaviour policies;

o consider a range of practical ideas to help the child in a highly realistic, positive way;

o draw you all together to follow a consistent, firm and supportive approach.

Raising self-esteem and morale of staff – a shared vision

At the heart of our work is the understanding that the welfare of your team is paramount to your school's success. This training day:

o gives ideas about how to look after yourself and develop respect and trust;

o offers you motivational strategies to deal with children and adults who challenge us at a fundamental level;

o helps you identify and evaluate your own energy levels;

o helps to create a work/life balance.

Advanced Quality Circle Time – reviewing and re-energising

This day is suitable for those who have acquired the necessary skills and introduced some Circle Time strategies, and now want to build on these.

The aims of the course are to:

o broaden and increase the scope and add new 'branches' of ideas to the established 'trunk' of the model;

o learn more exciting games and creative ideas;

o support the further development of children's social skills, imagination and emotional literacy.

Parents and staff evenings – broadening the vision

Parents and schools must work together as partners, and share the same ideals. This session helps parents to:

o learn about positive strategies that can be maintained not only throughout the school day but throughout the child's/pupil's whole life;

o give parents further insights into what the school is hoping to achieve;

o enter into the same proactive behaviour policy as the staff.

Best value three-day training package

The consultancy is engaged in a number of specific programmes, special tailor-made projects for schools and LEAs. Here are some examples:

o circles of support for Year 10 pupils who are at risk of crime and disaffection;

o helping LEAs implement our two-day programme in primary schools;

o turning round schools in difficulty with a structured training programme.

Train the trainers

Individuals delivering courses within our model should be accredited through a week-long, intensive residential course.

The Quality Circle Time model may lose its strength and purpose if implemented by personnel who have not been accredited. Our in-depth courses equip individuals with the underlying philosophy and psychology to train others. Past experience has shown our success in inspiring individuals and changing the culture within a whole community. We have run these five-day in-depth courses for the past fourteen years. They enable the attendees to return to their schools or LEAs to teach others. Delegates have been drawn from a number of different areas of education.

This course also enables delegates to gain a certificate of Further Professional Studies from the University of Bristol. After accreditation, you are required to complete a 6,000 word assignment which is an award in its own right and also carries thirty credit points towards an M.Ed. or Advanced Diploma in Education. The M.Ed. programme includes routes to professional training in educational psychology recognised by the British Psychological Society.

Additional courses from Jenny Mosley Consultancies

o Peer mediation
o Children beyond – drugs education
o Bridging the circle – working on successful transition
o Boost your energy
o Switching children on to learning
o Relaxation training for all
o Children and staff

- o NLP foundation skills
- o Creative arts training days for all
- o More than splish, splash, splosh
- o Sound, move and make – integrating arts media
- o Lifting the spirits
- o The art of storytelling
- o Power of puppets
- o Bring drama into your Circle Time
- o Developing a holistic approach to emotional health – creating the work/life balance
- o Conference days
- o After dinner speakers
- o 'Train the trainers' for your own local education authority

How to afford our training

Sources of funding for individuals include:

- o Headlamp
- o PSHE Advisory Service
- o DfES – Social, Emotional & Behavioural Skills (SEBS)
- o Career development loan
- o individual teacher bursaries for Continuing Professional Development

---

Jenny Mosley's work in schools can lead to a profound re-orientation of thinking at grassroots level, and in terms of enhanced pupil performance is likely to prove an excellent investment.

Professor David Fontana, Distinguished Visiting Fellow, Cardiff University

---

The Maplesdon Noakes School identified the Jenny Mosley Consultancies Whole School Quality Circle Time as an exciting model to play a major role in delivering the vision of a whole school policy for self-esteem.

Douglas Kimber, Headteacher, Maplesdon Noakes School, Maidstone, Kent (2000). (This school was designated by the DfES the second most improved school in the country.)

Research available

Since Jenny Mosley developed her particular approach eighteen years ago there have been several in-depth studies into her work which reveal the positive effects of our training. These are available on request.

For further information about training please call our team; we will help and advise you on finding the courses that suit your needs.

A collection of ideas to consider

o Share your training day with a cluster.
o Host training in your school, sell places to delegates in other schools and charge them fees.
o Contact local Beacon schools as sometimes they will pay for training.
o DfES standards site – www.dfes.standards.gov.uk
o Behaviour Improvement Programmes (BIP).
o Contact your local LEA about Behaviour Education Support Teams and Sporting Playgrounds.
o Local healthy schools teams.
o Excellence in Cities.
o Connexions.
o European Social Funding.
o Charities.
o Hold a conference or training event on a Saturday to avoid having to arrange supply cover.

Positive Press resources catalogue

Telephone: 01225 767157
e-mail: circletime@jennymosley.co.uk
Write to: 28a Gloucester Road, Trowbridge, Wiltshire BA14 0AA
Visit our website: www.circle-time.co.uk